posh®

Coloring
BOOK

THOMAS KINKADE
Painter of Light

Andrews McMeel
Publishing®
a division of Andrews McMeel Universal

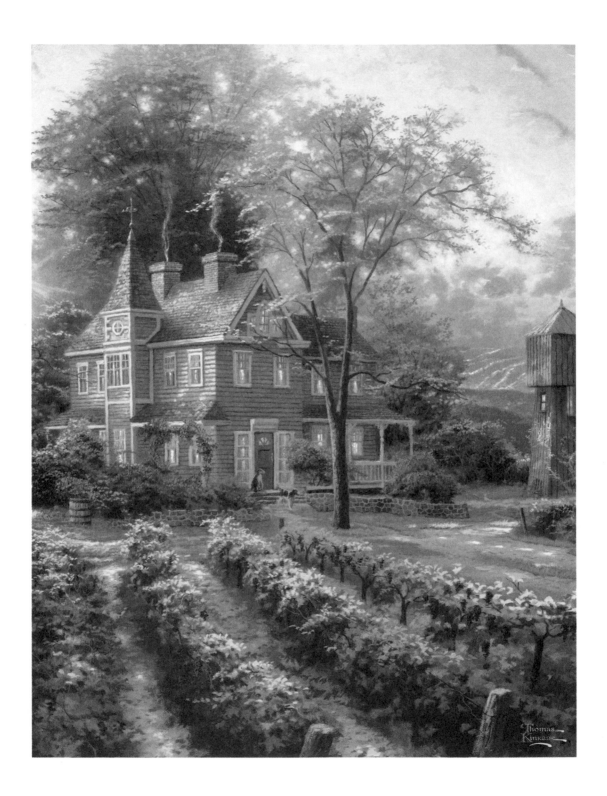

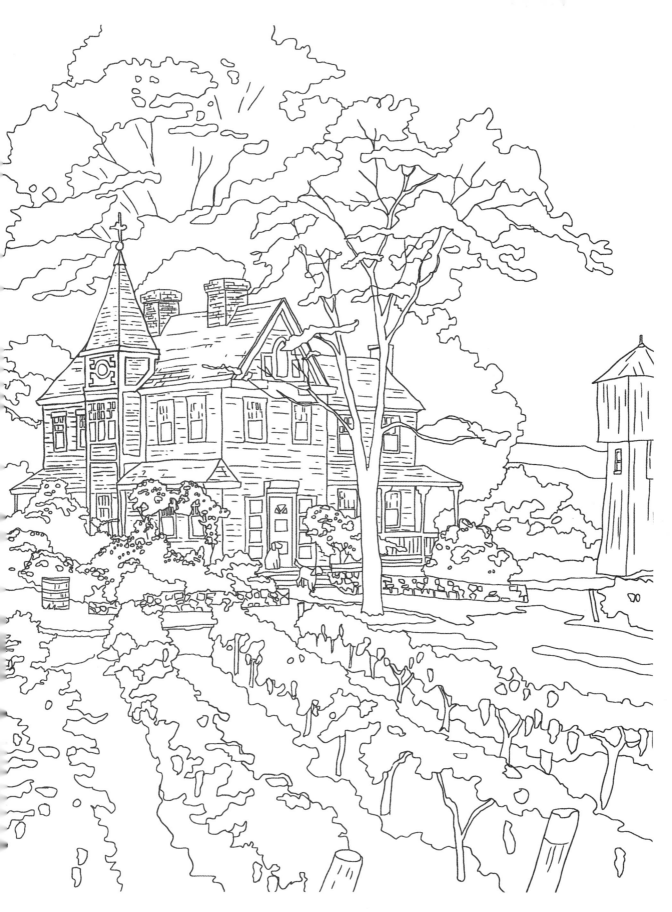

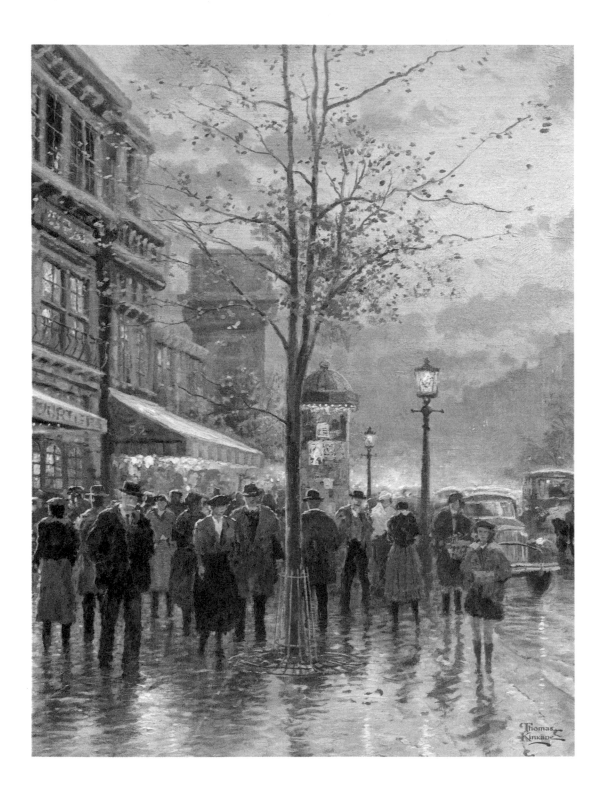

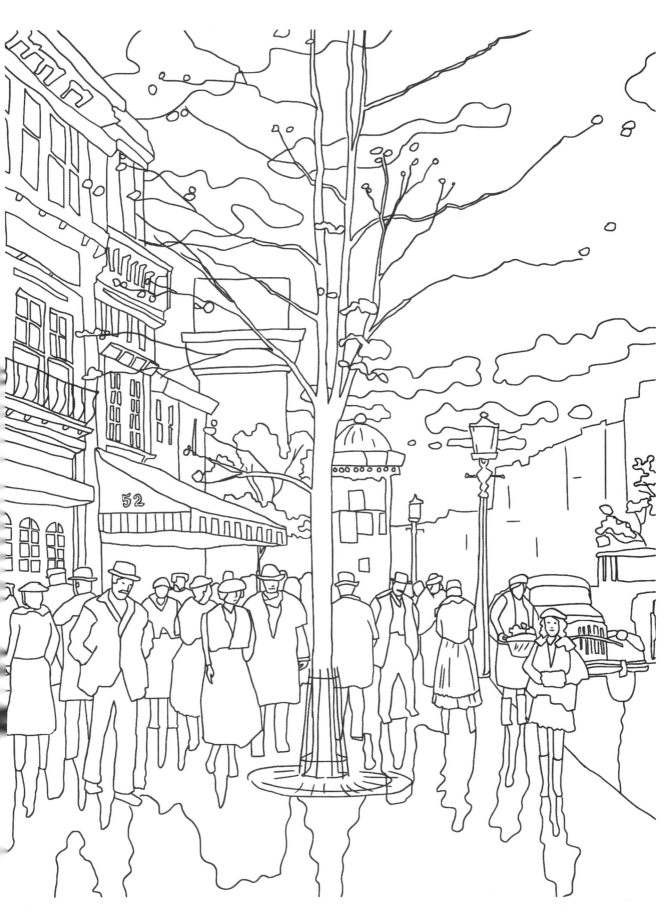

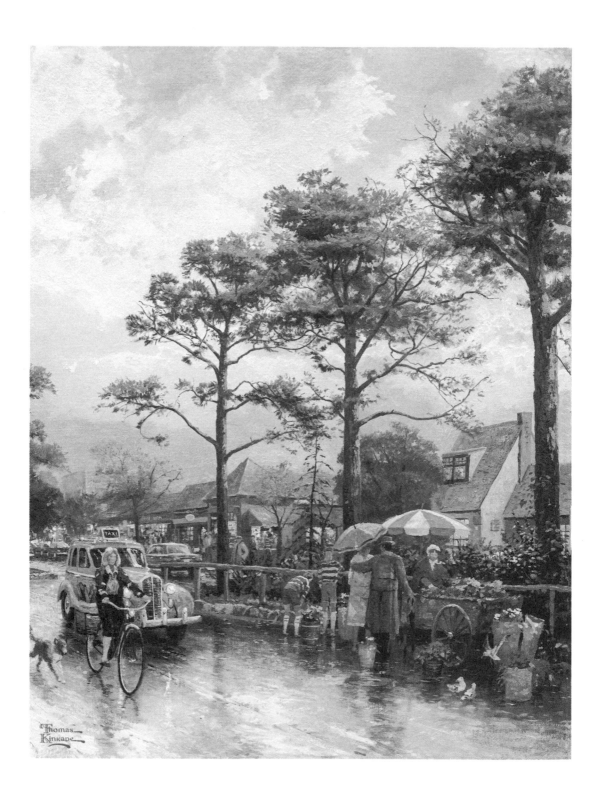

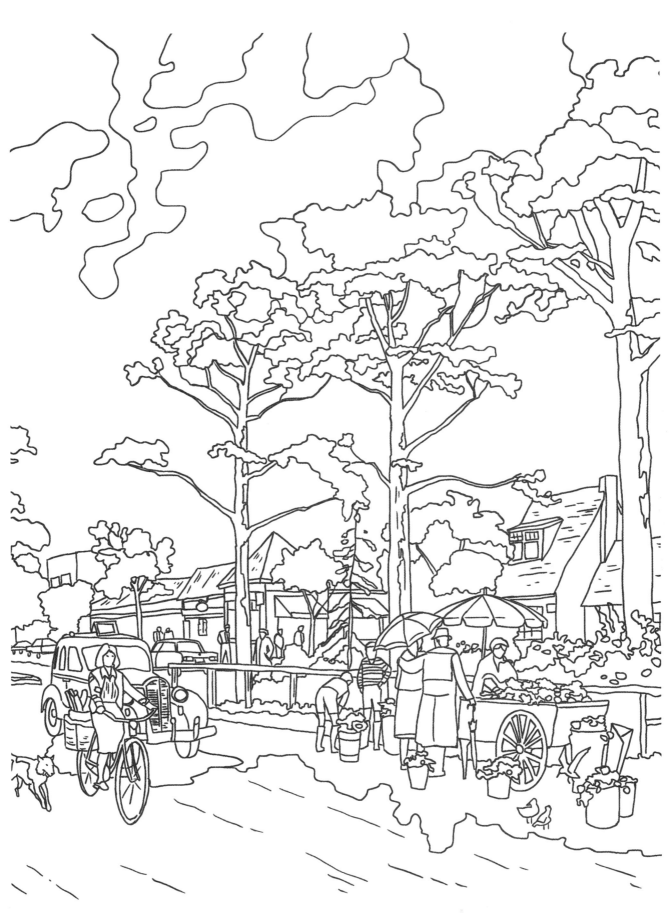

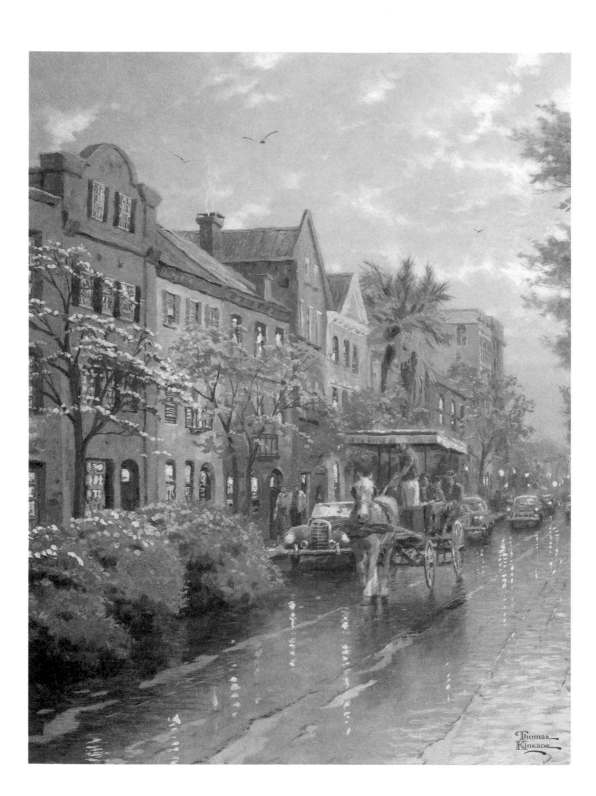

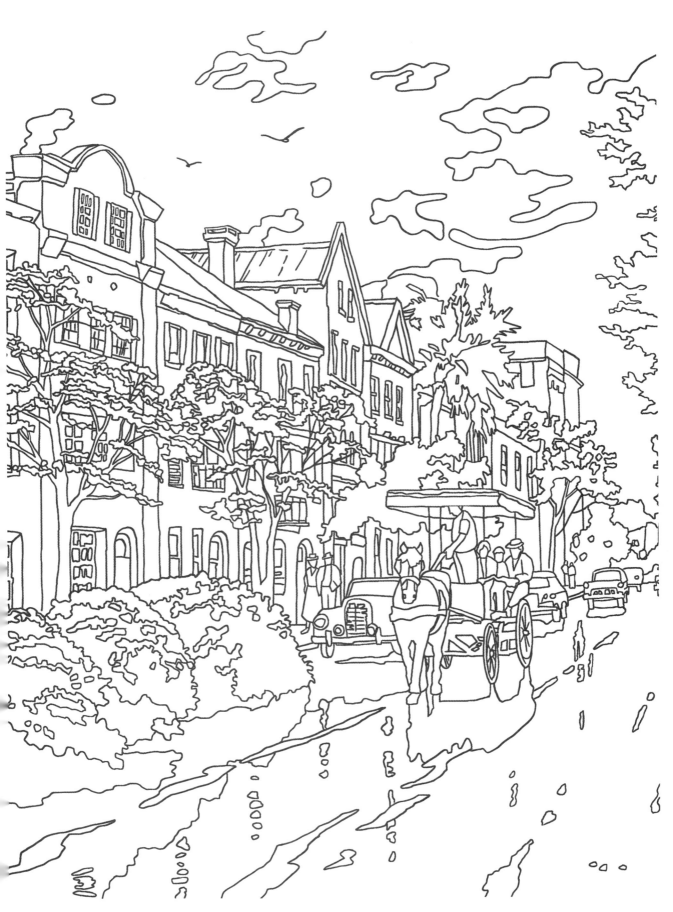

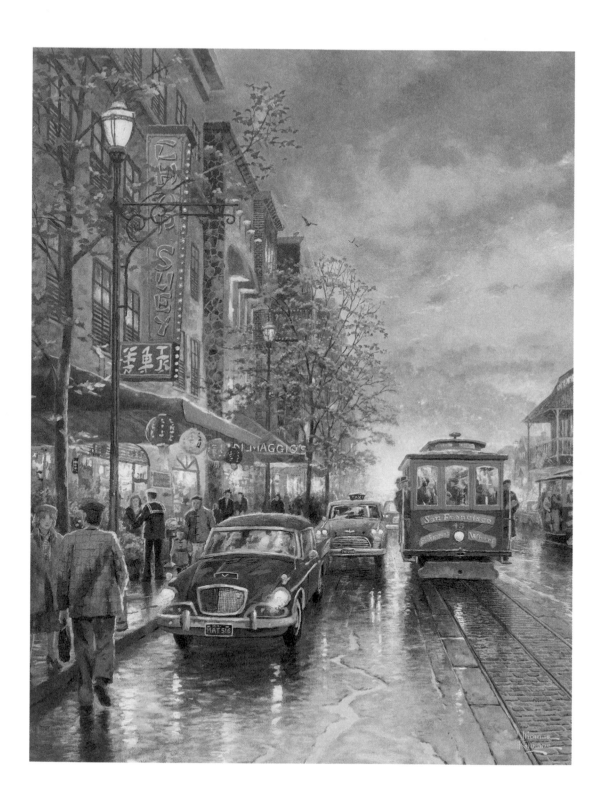

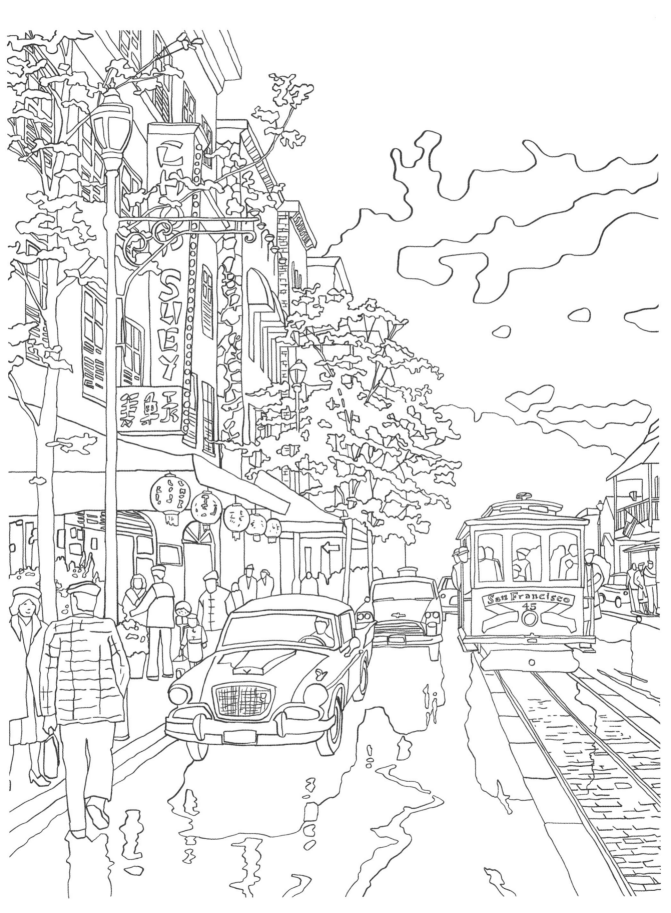

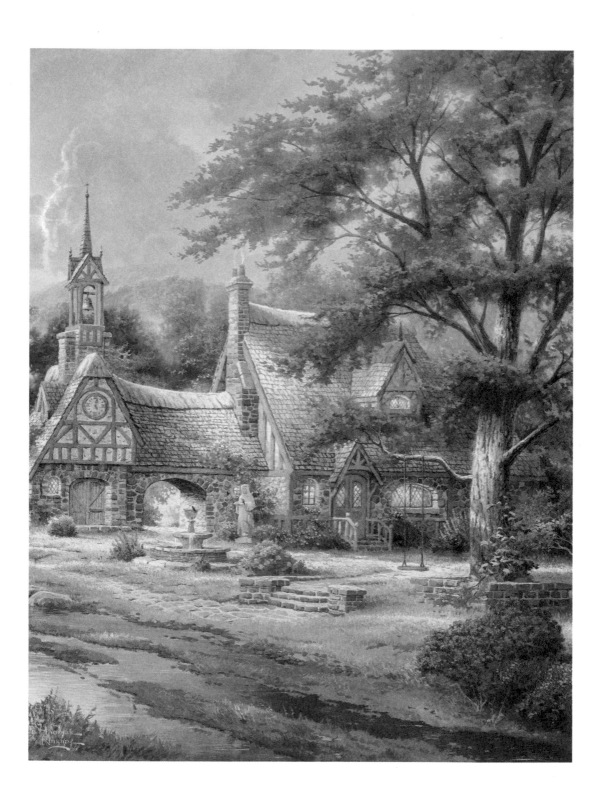

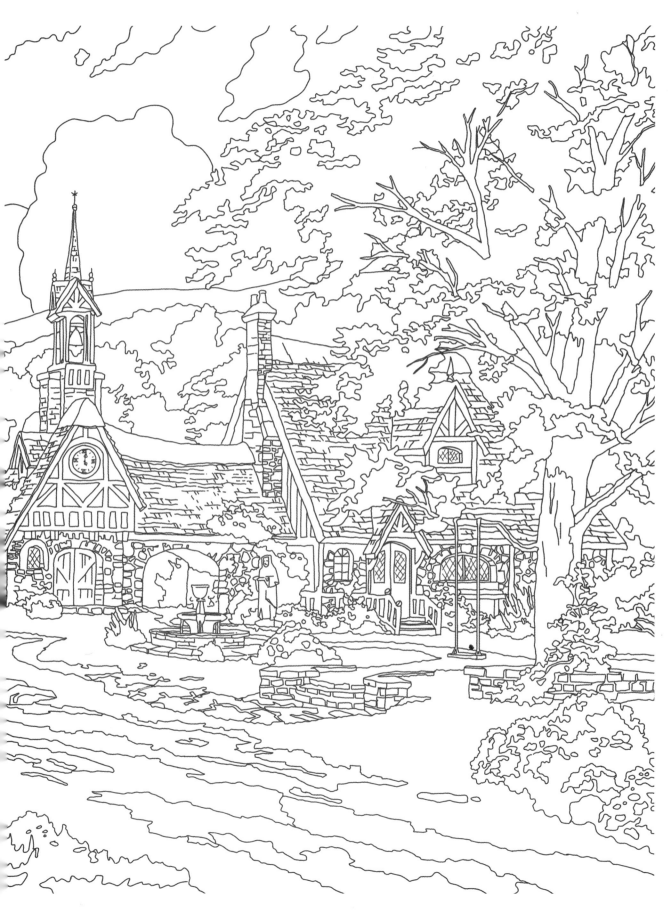

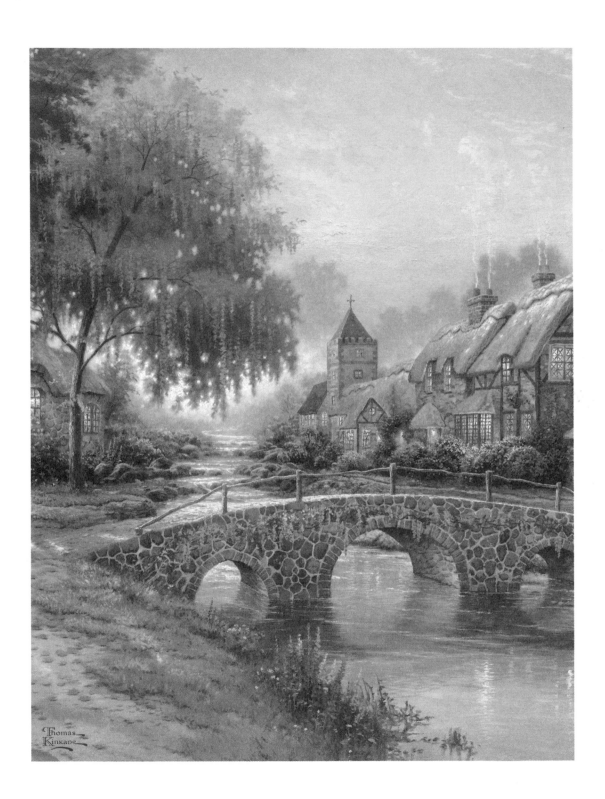

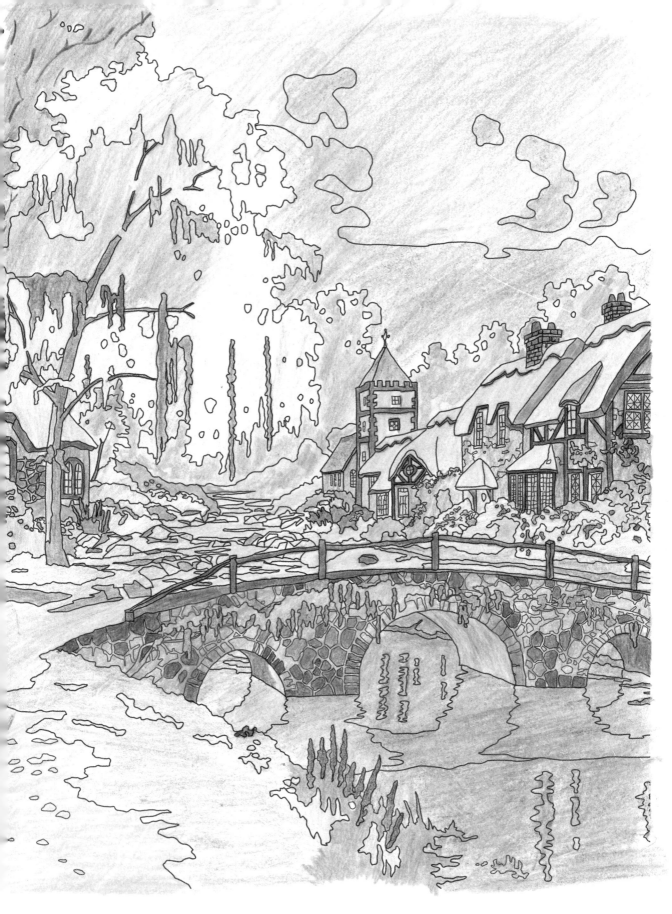

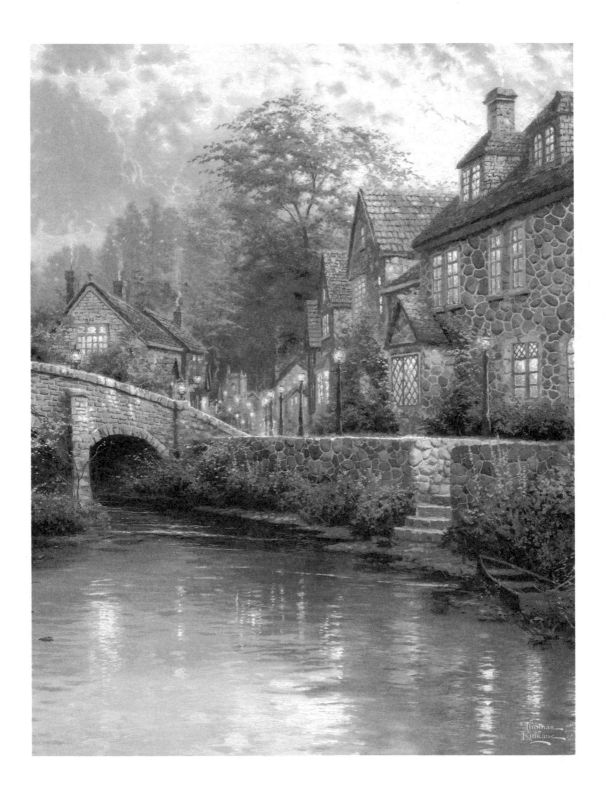

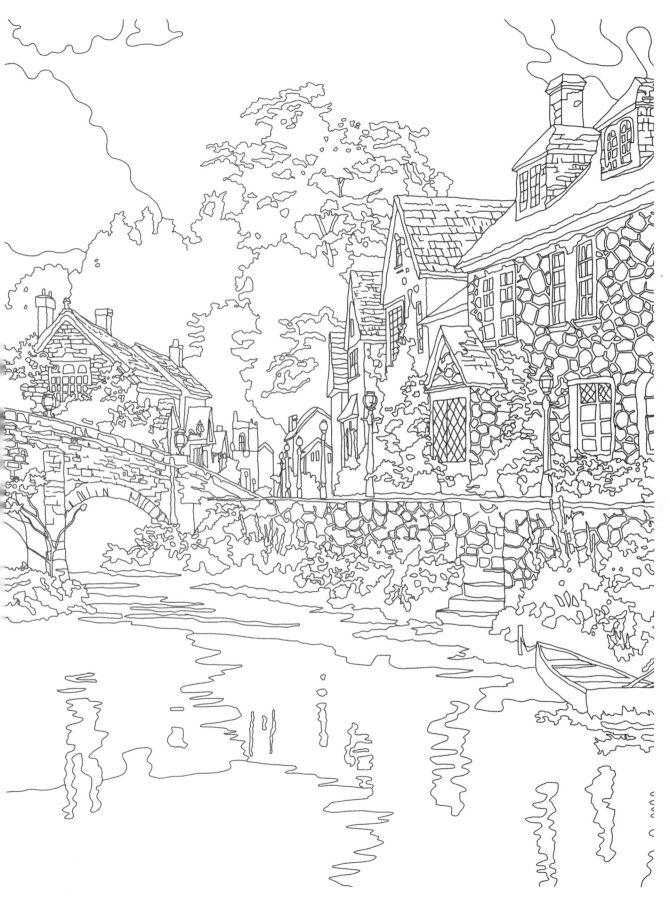

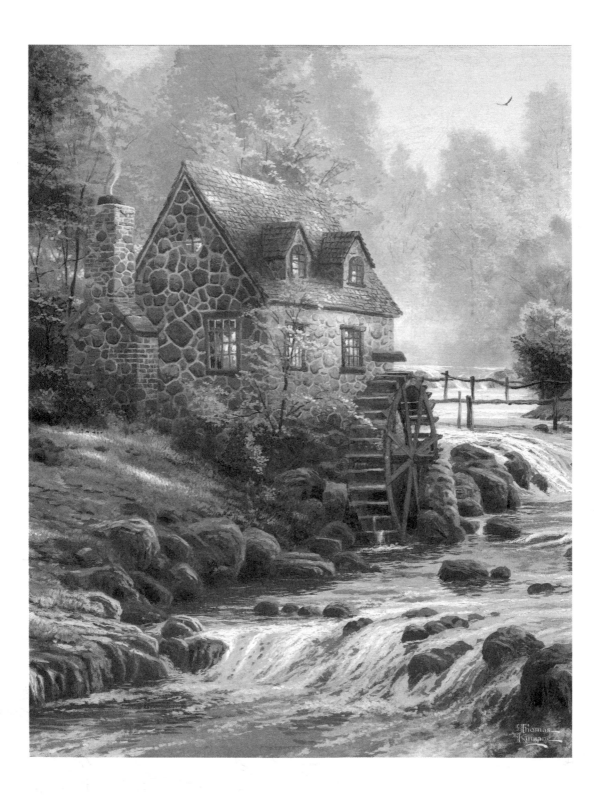

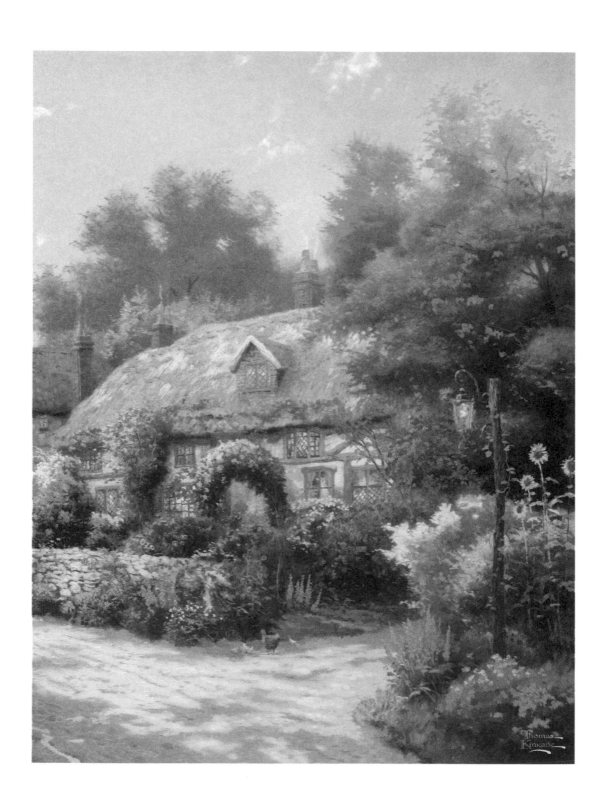

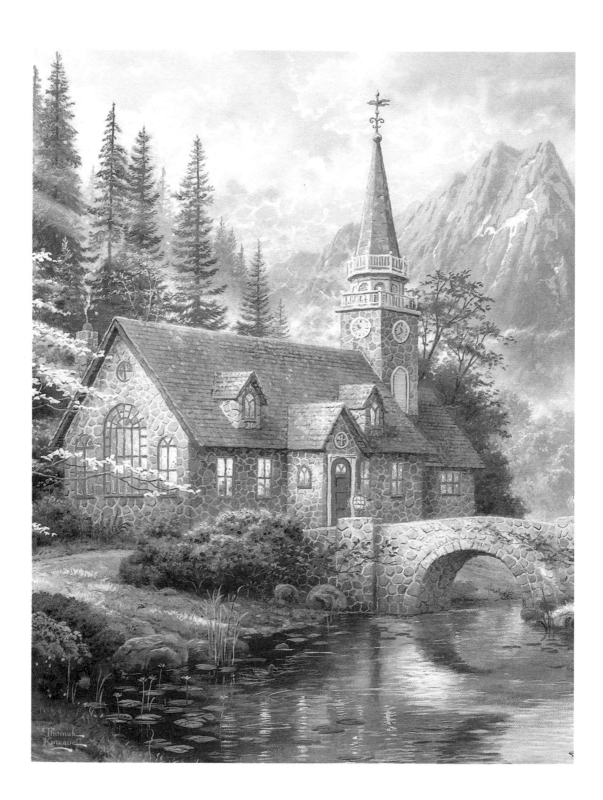

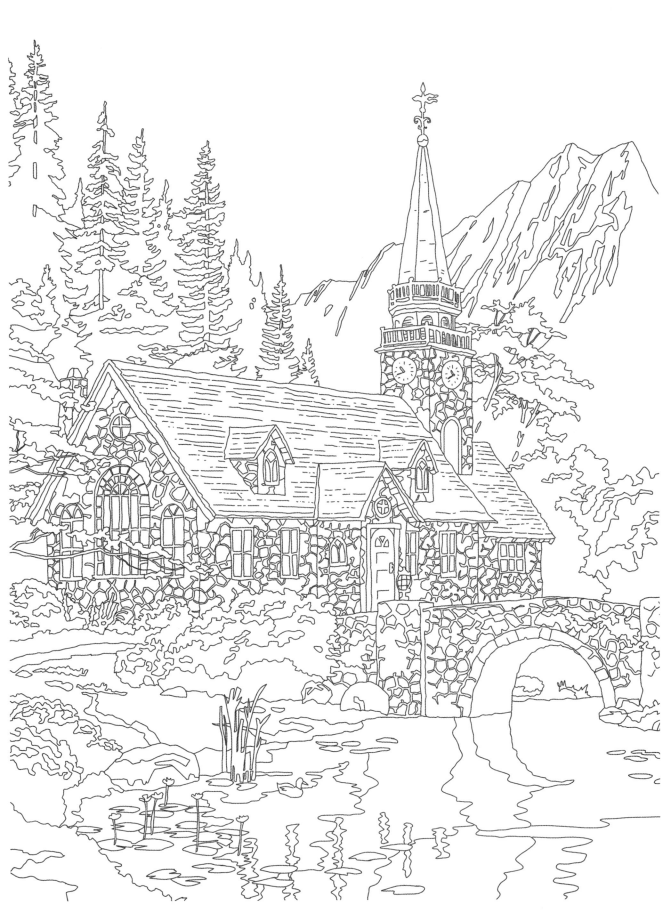

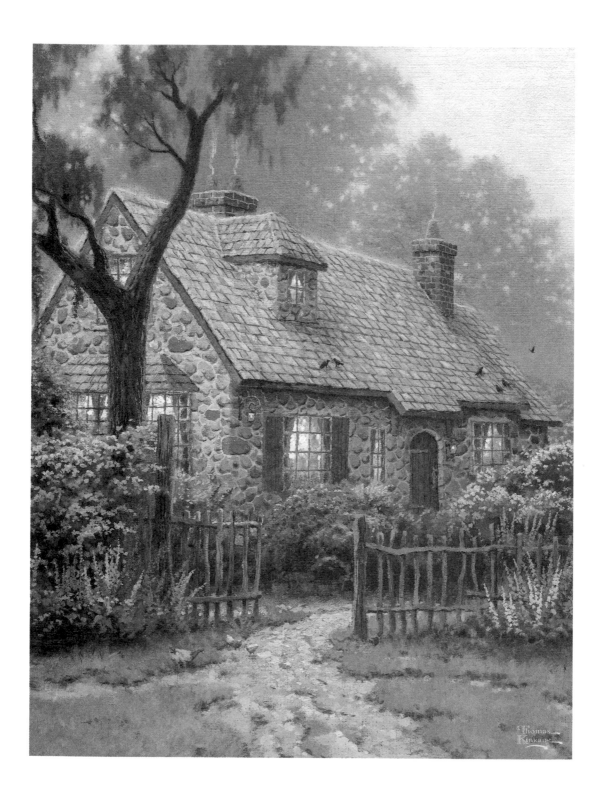

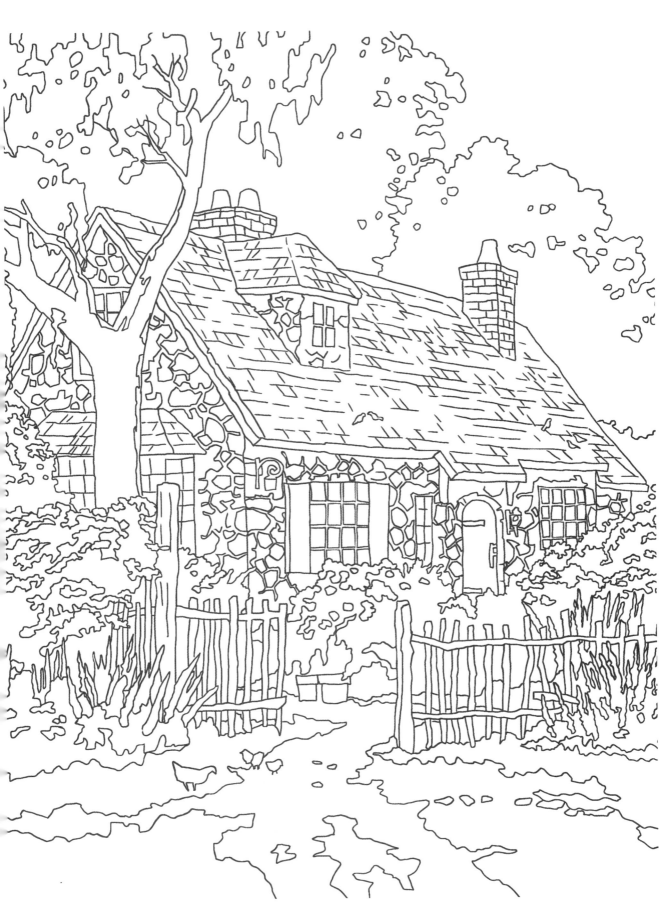

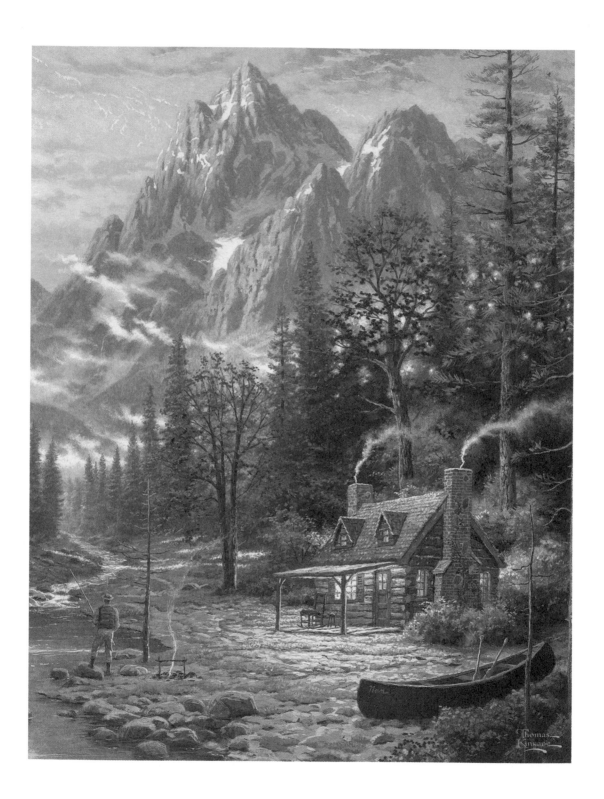

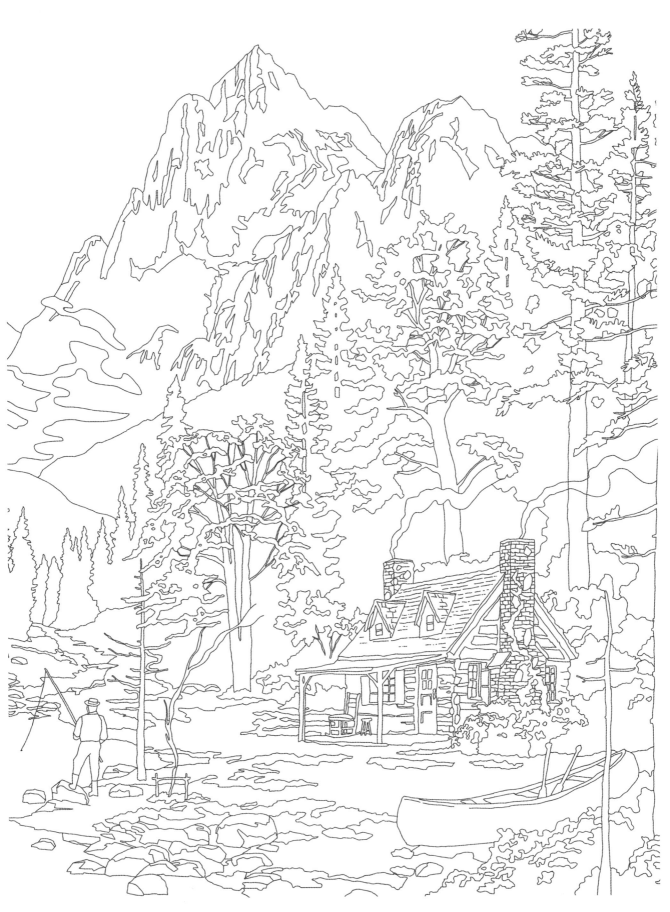

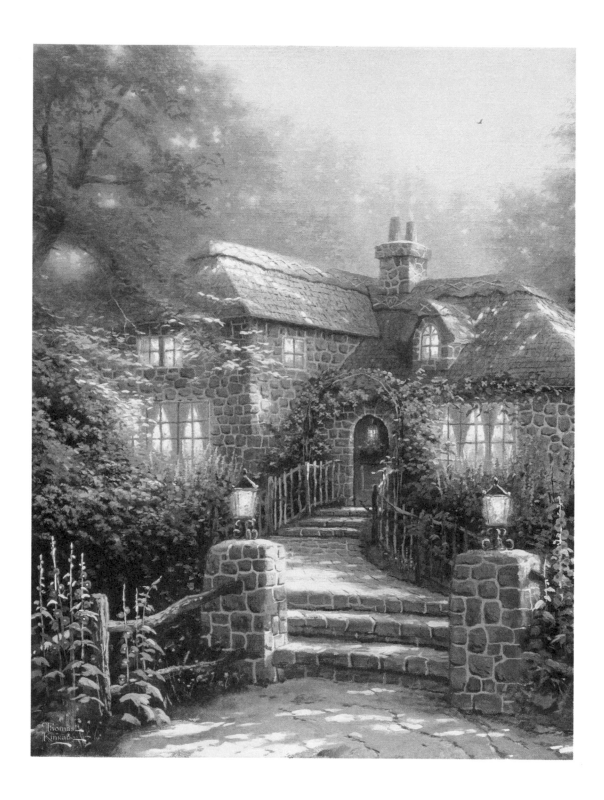

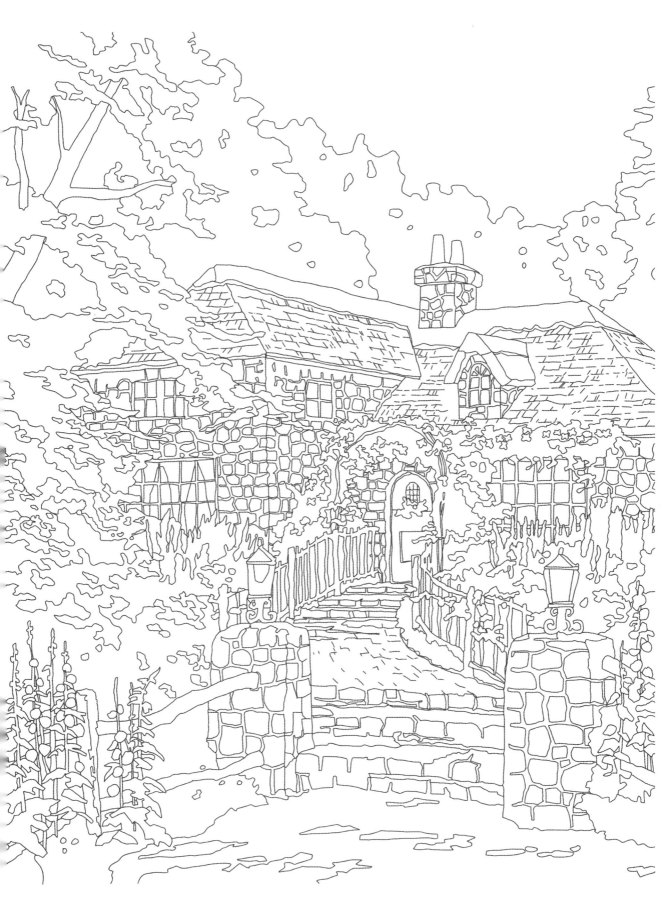

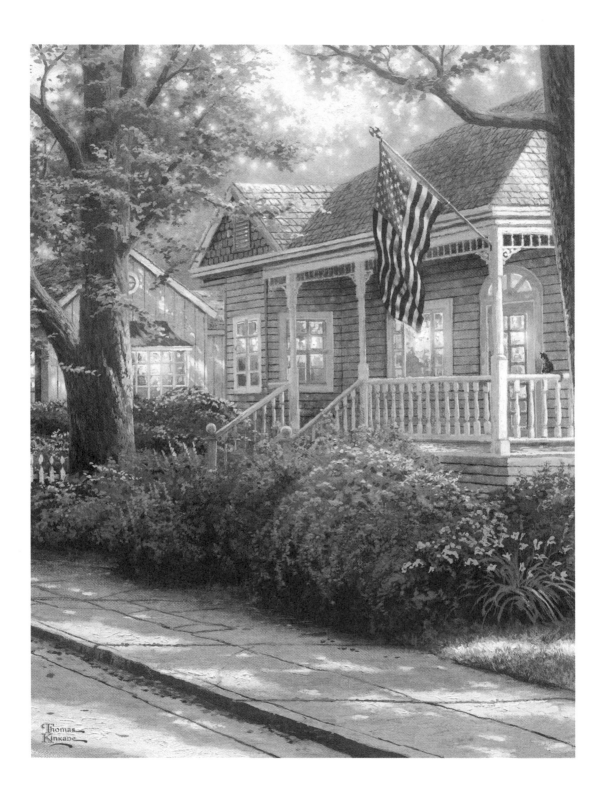

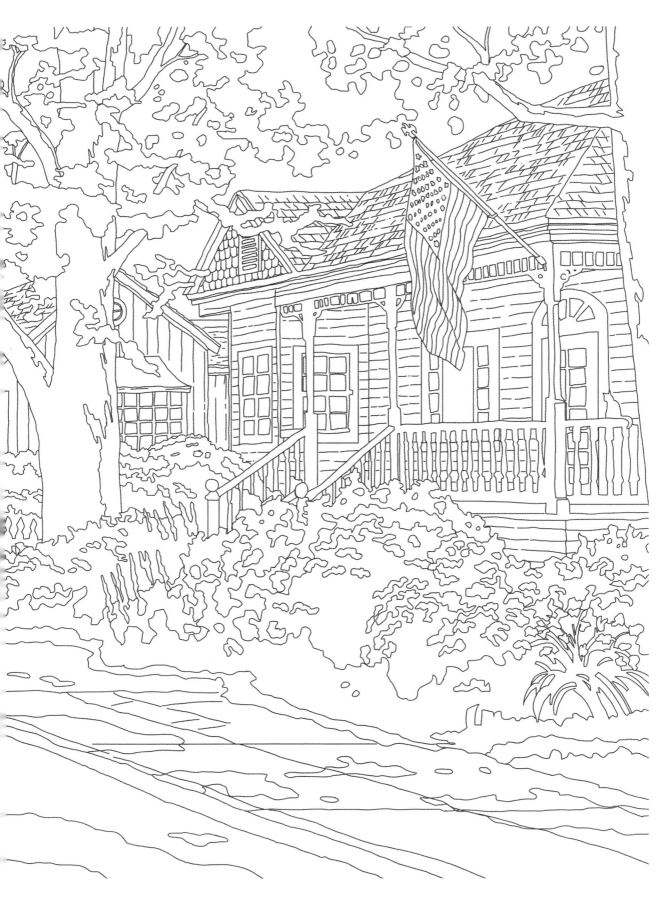

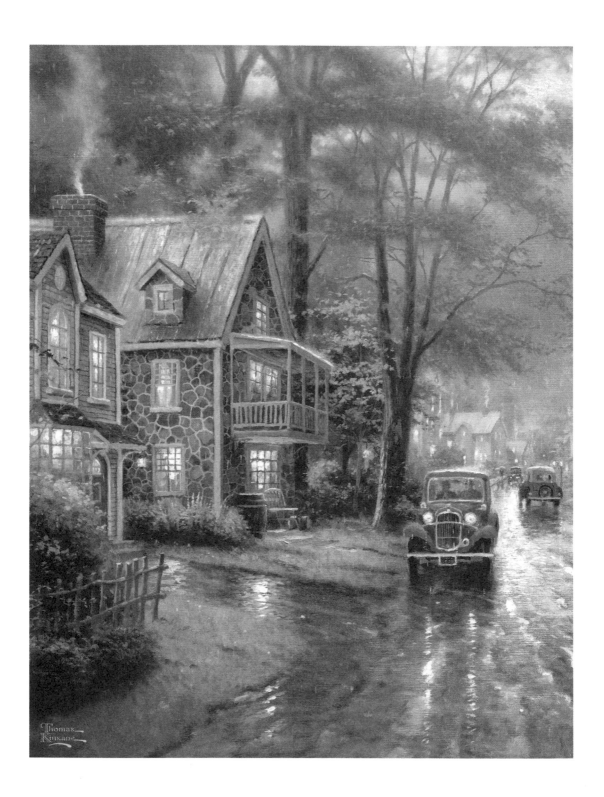

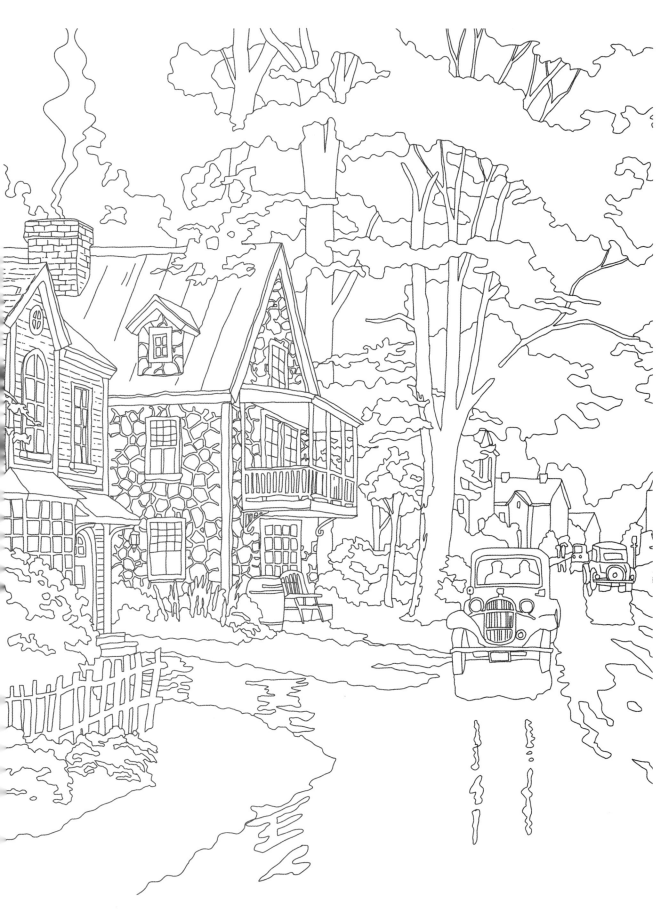

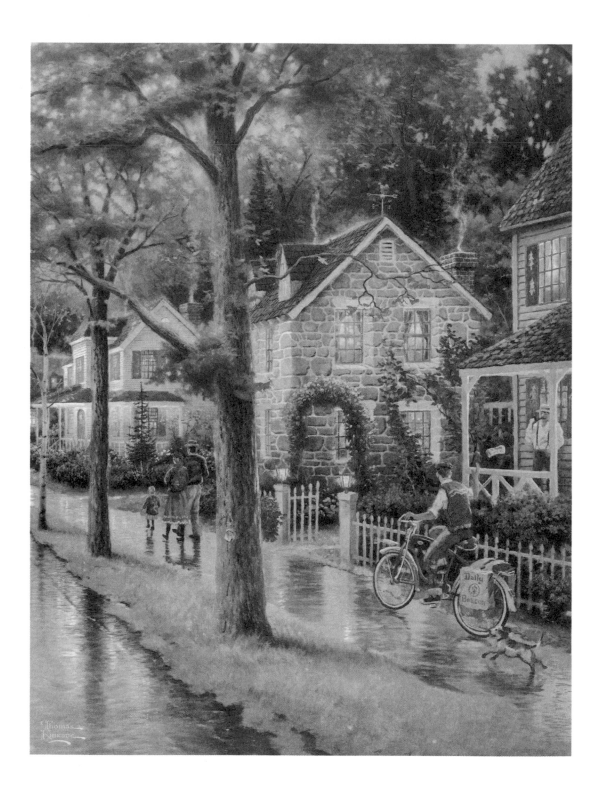

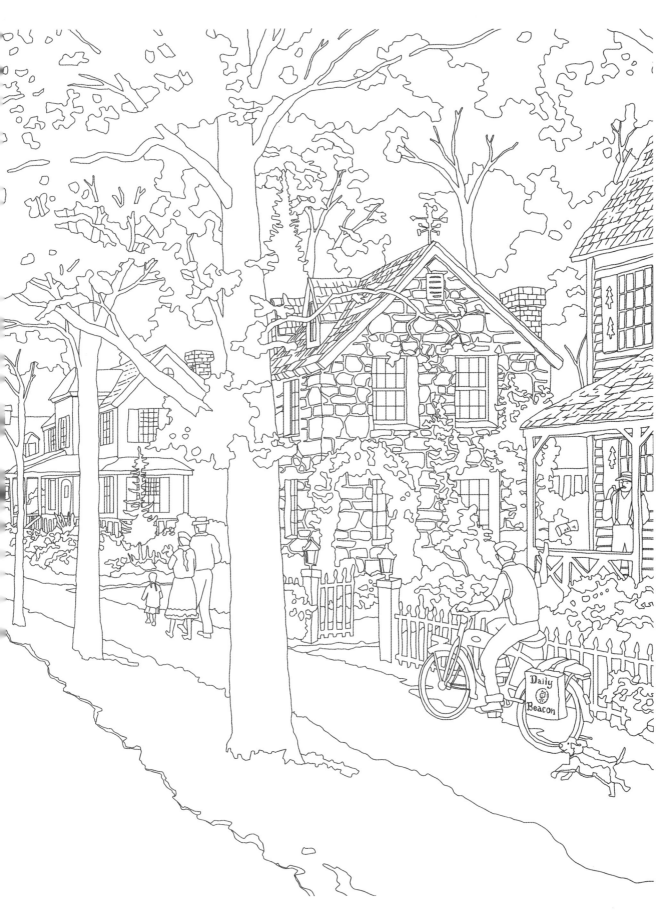

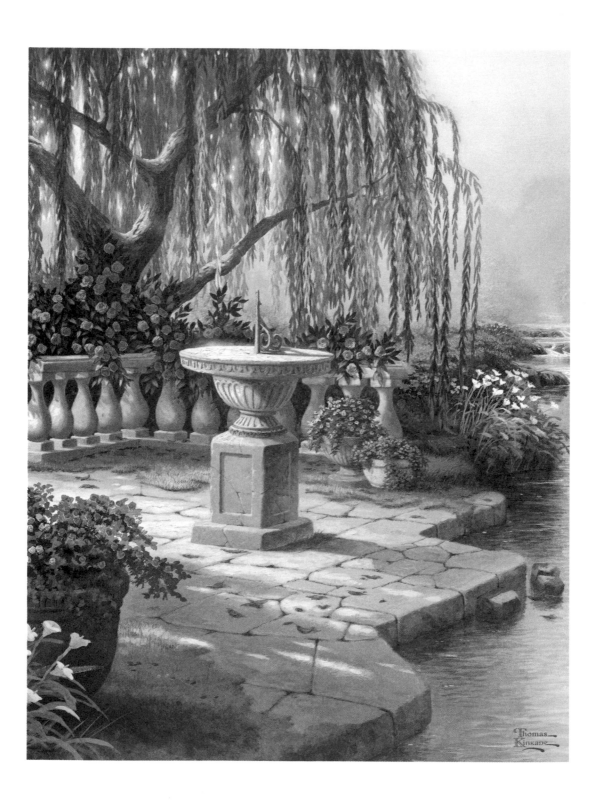

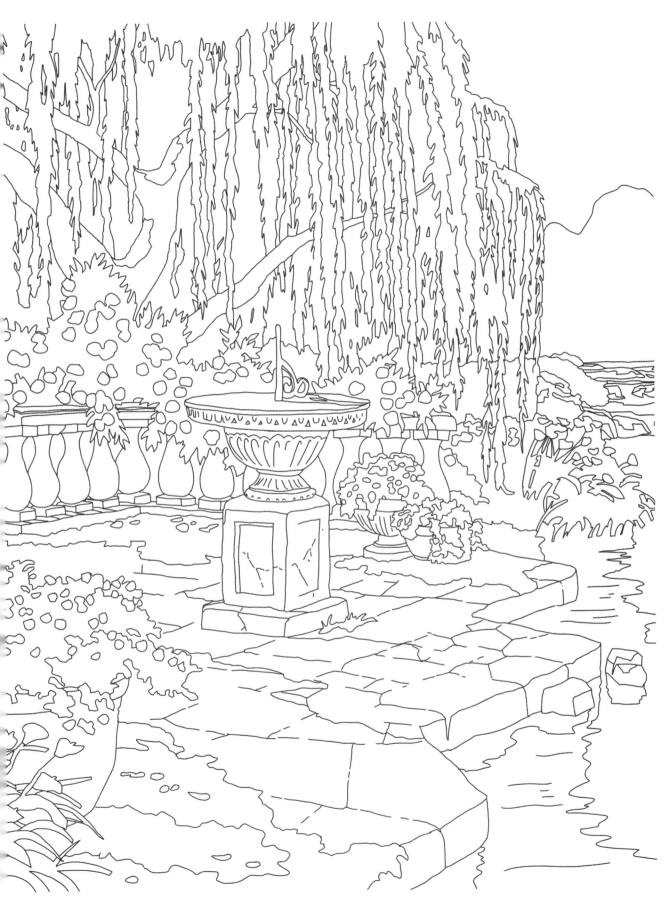

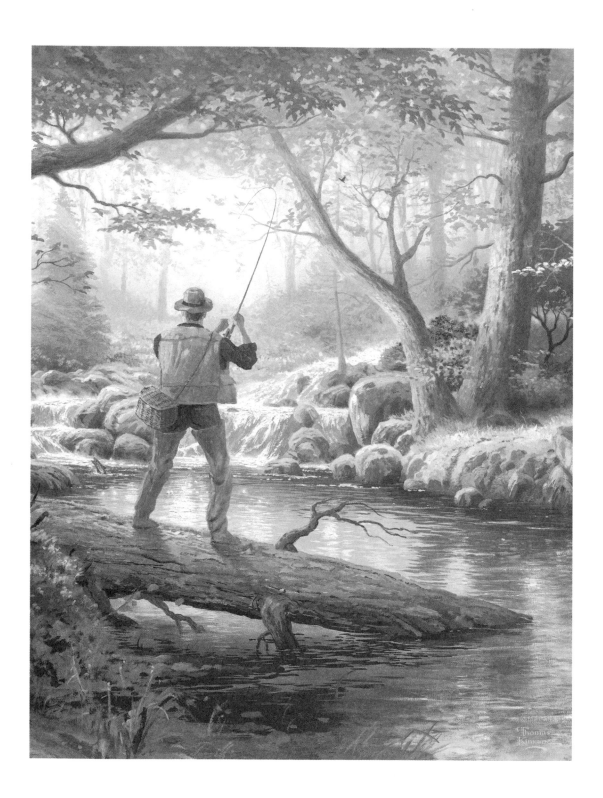

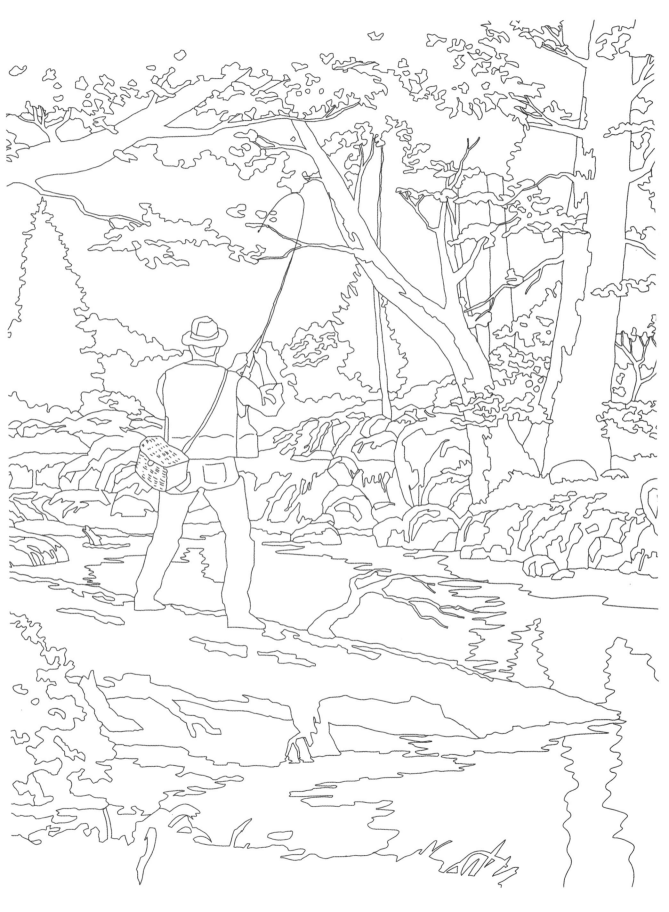

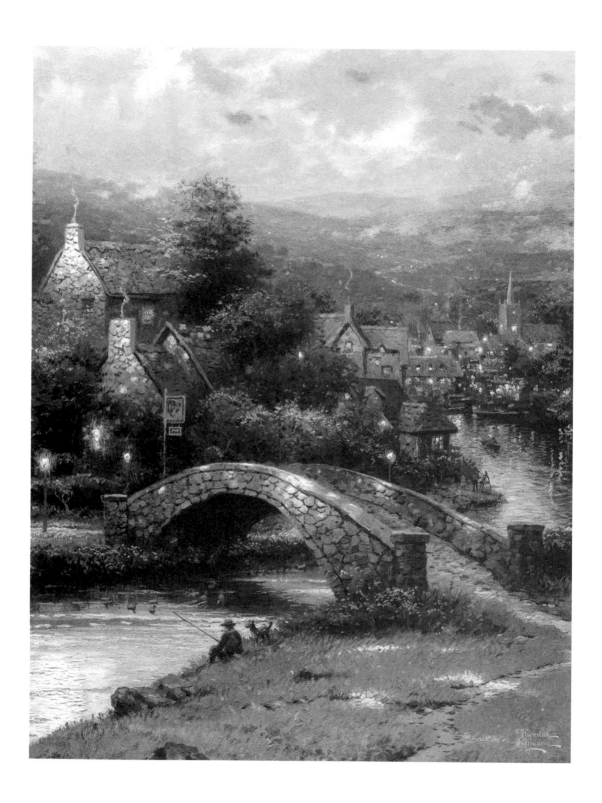

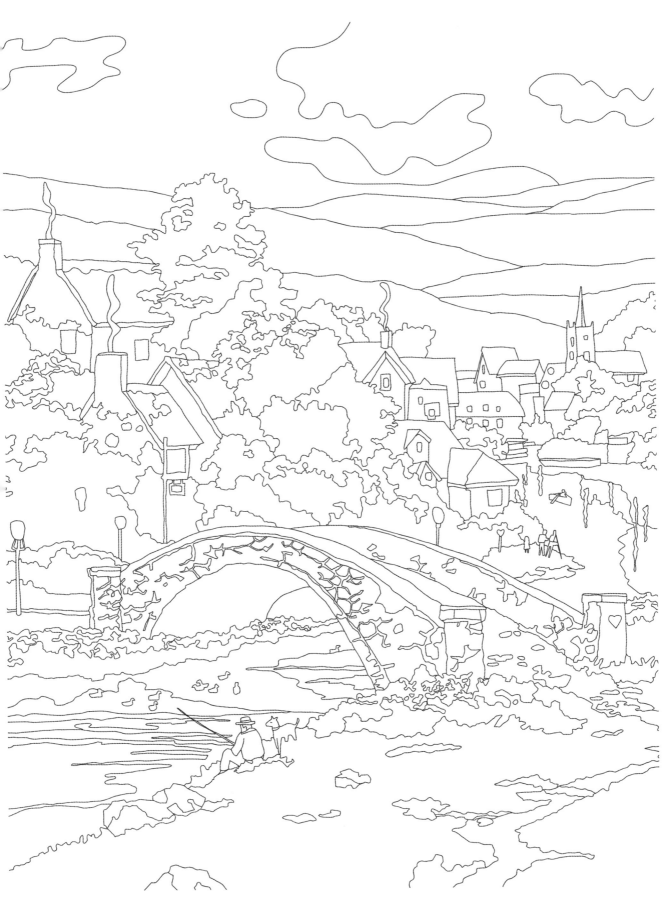

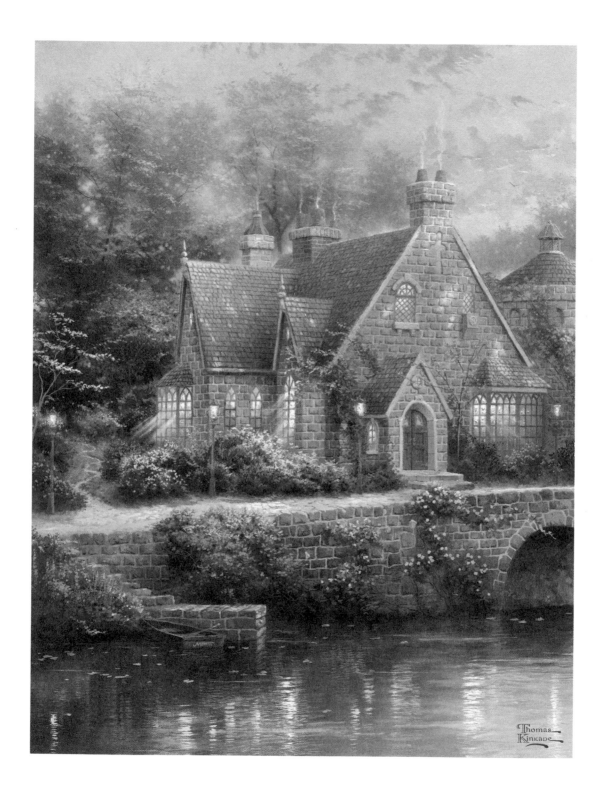

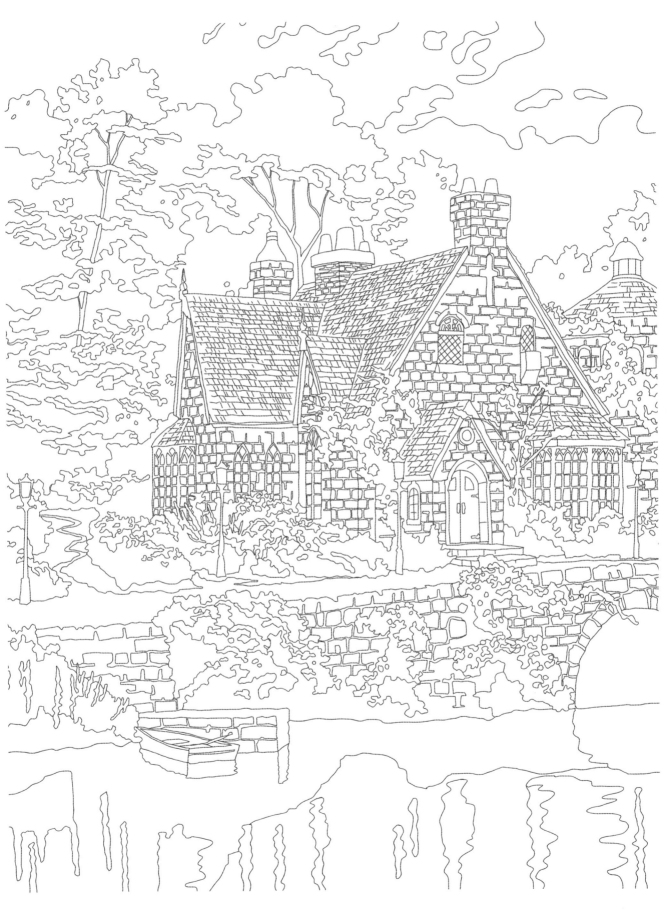

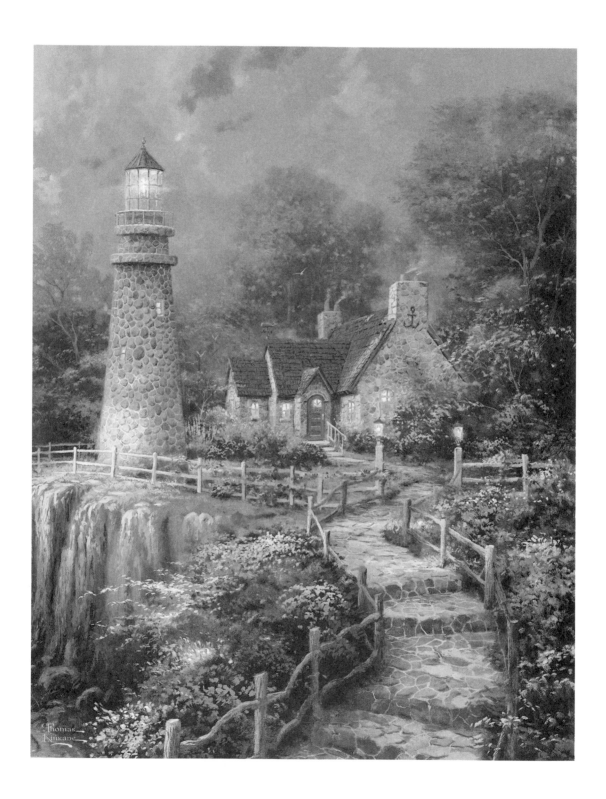

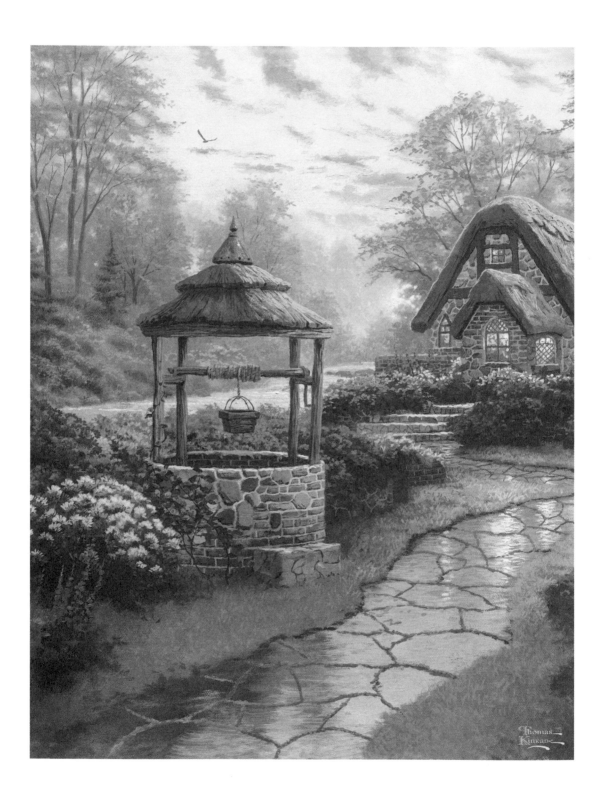

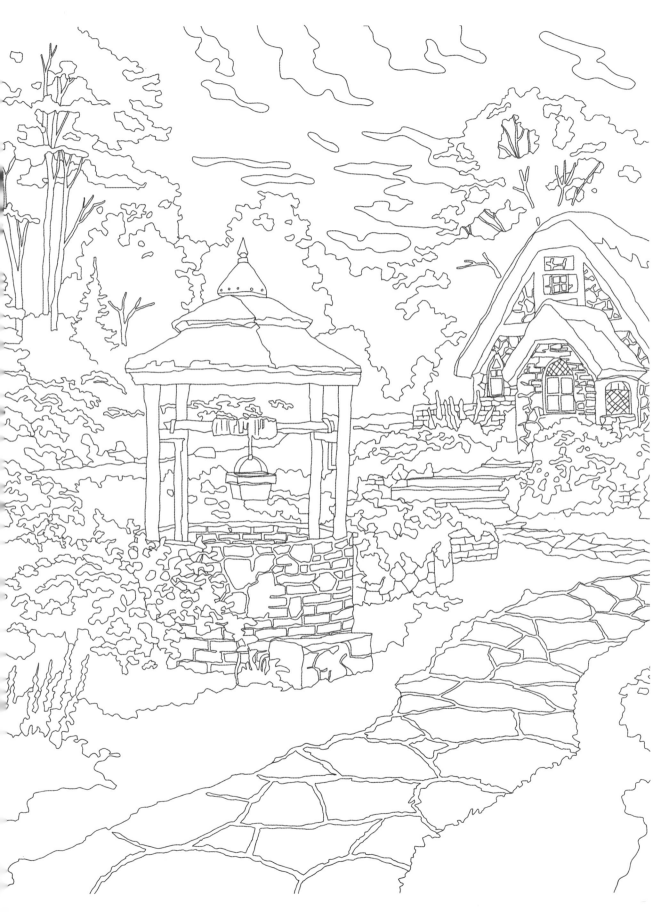

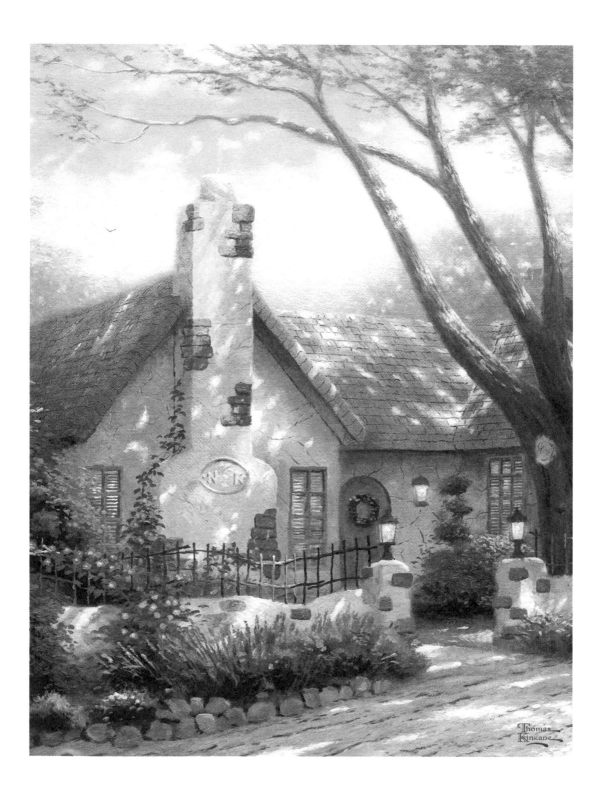

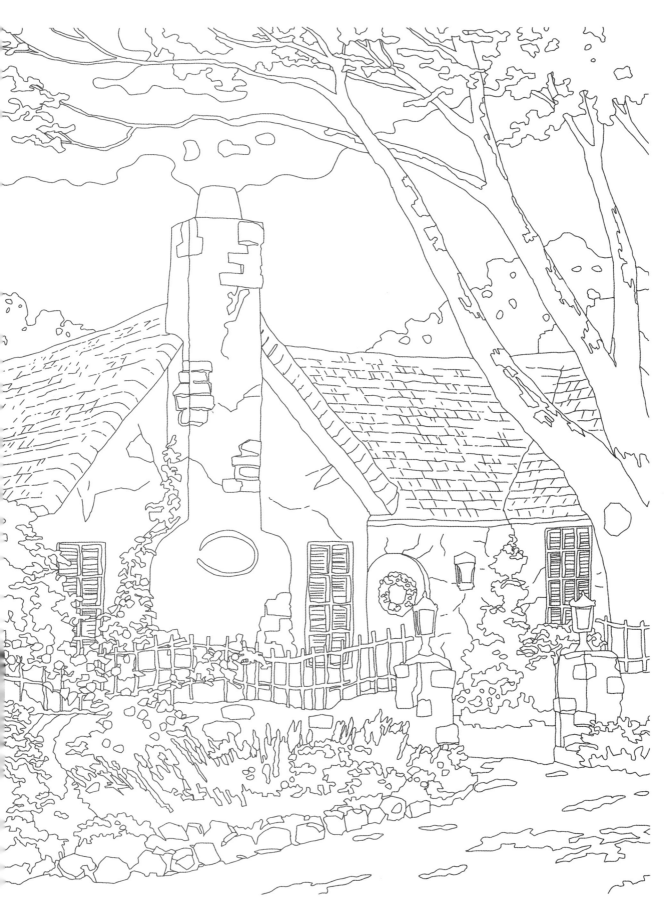

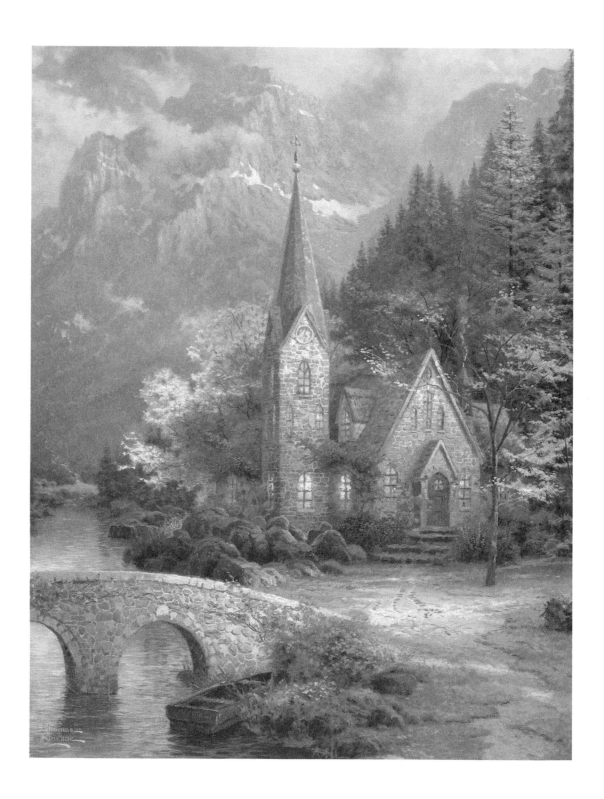

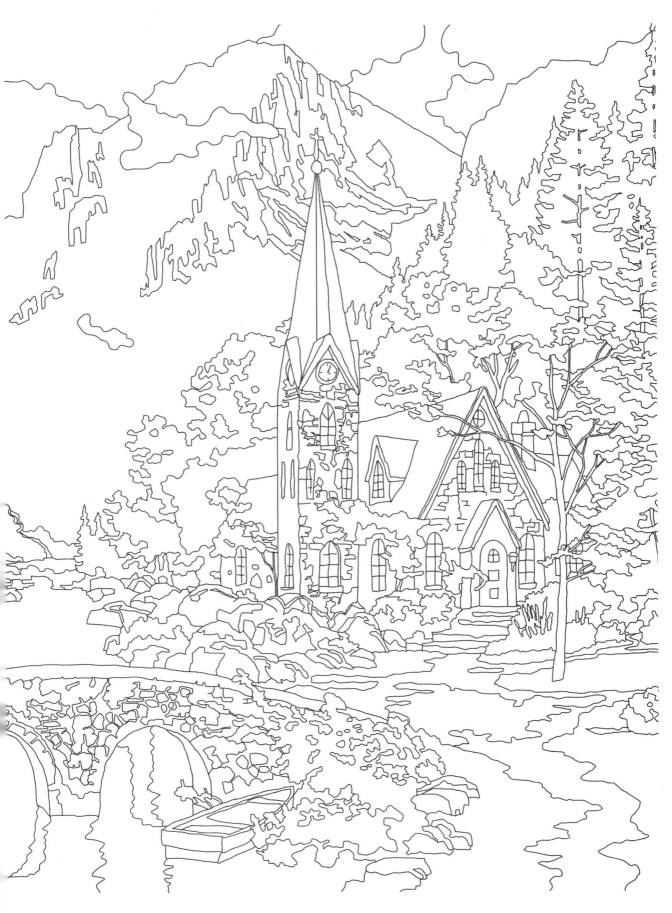

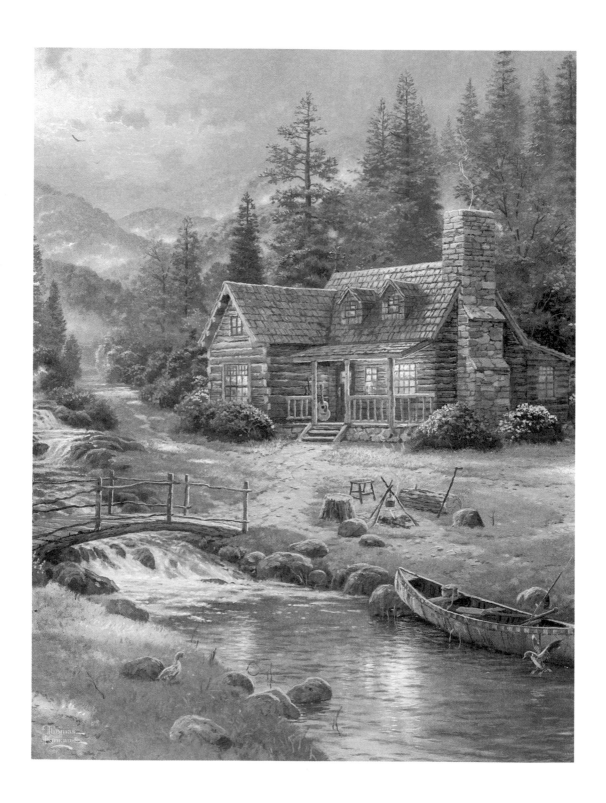

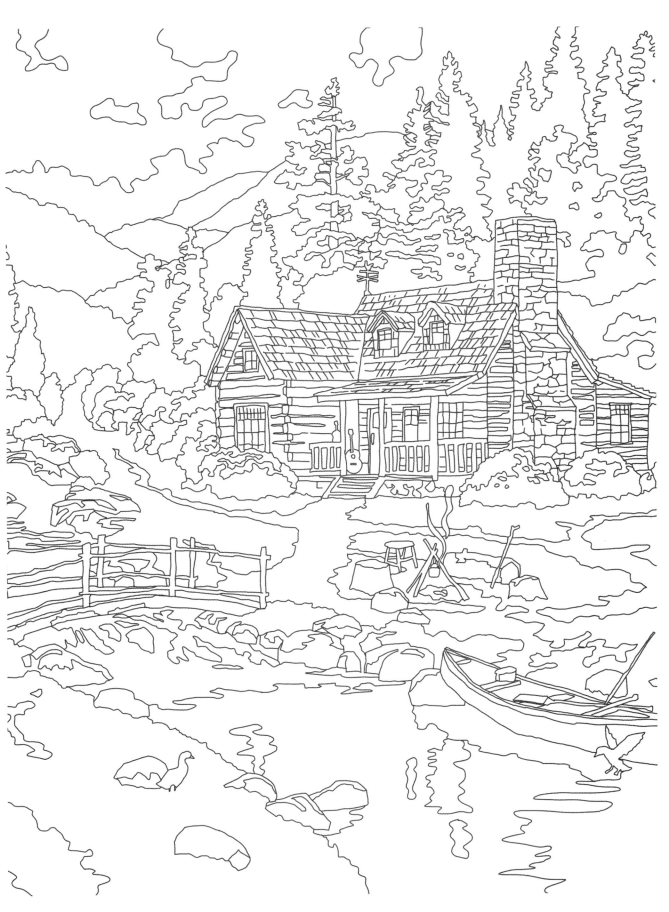

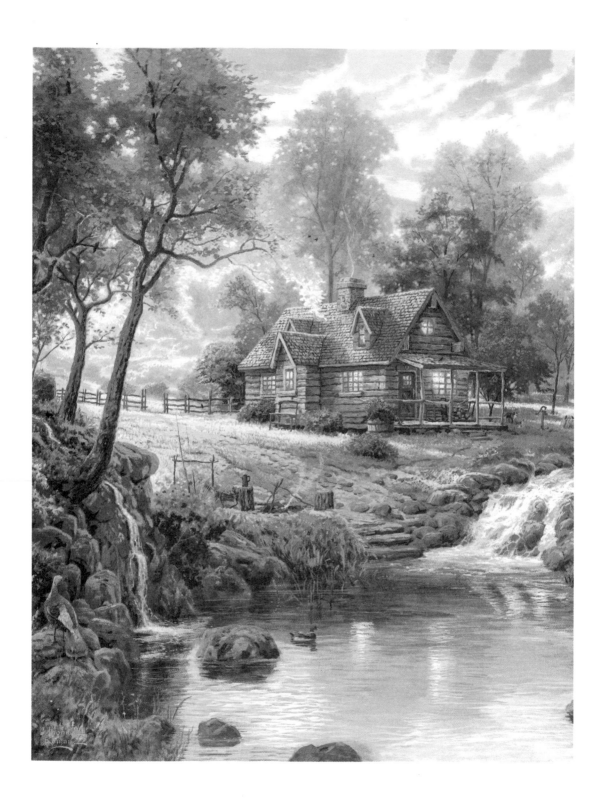

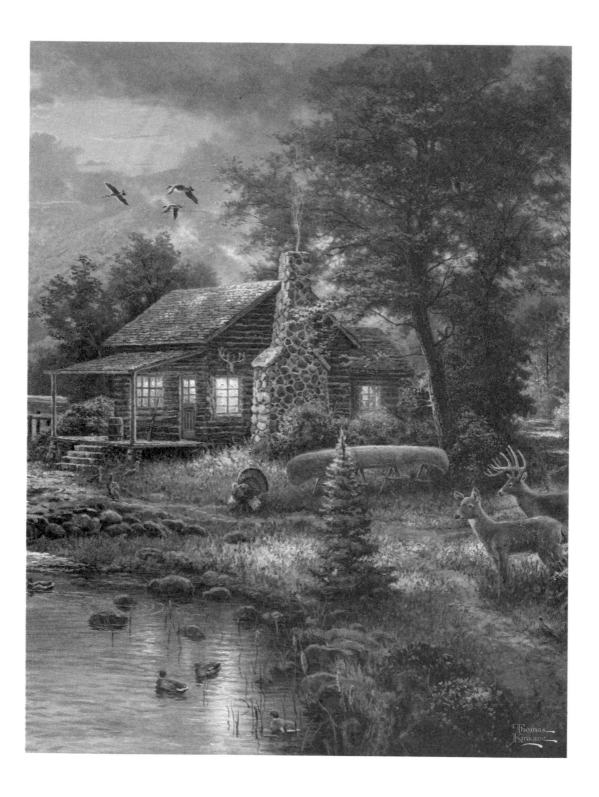

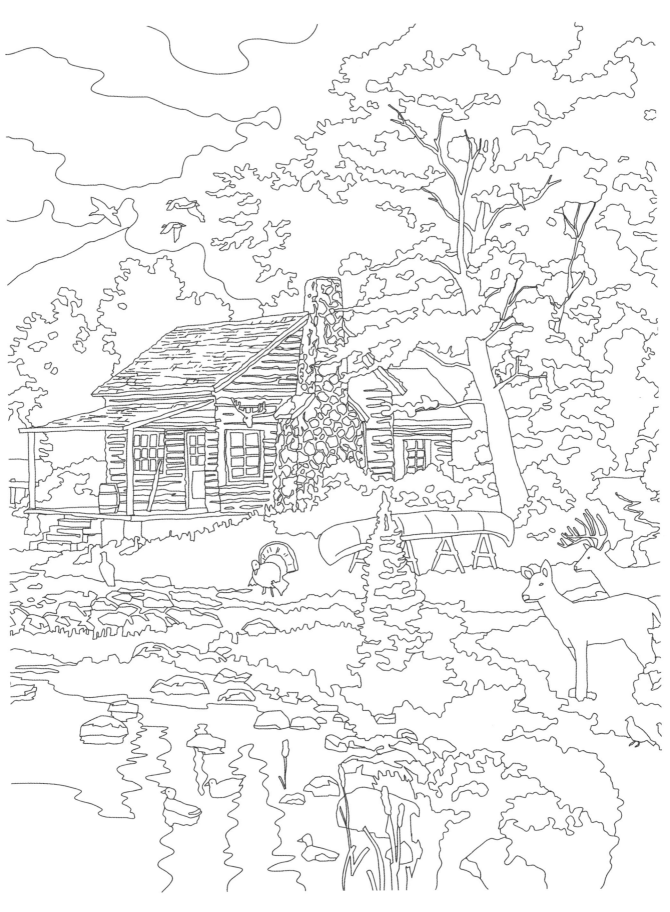

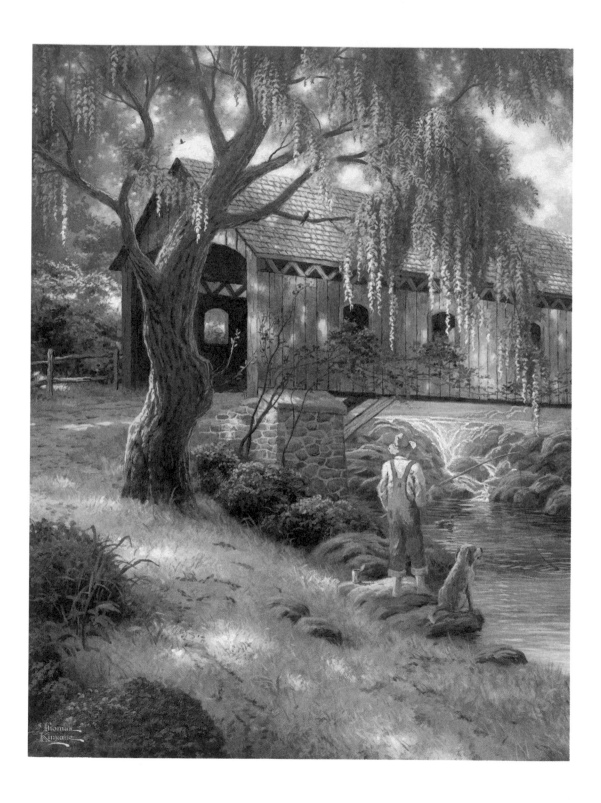

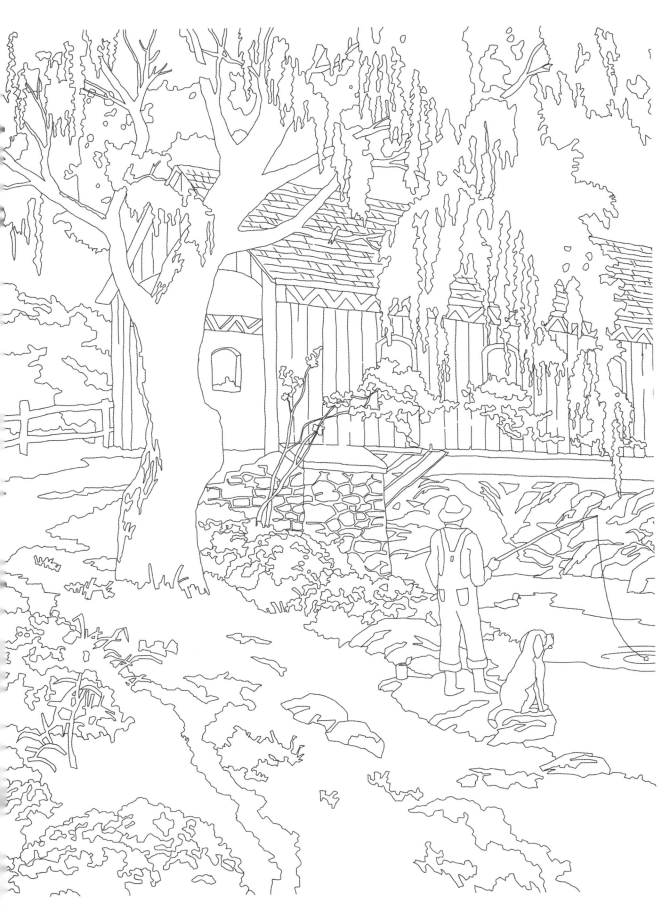

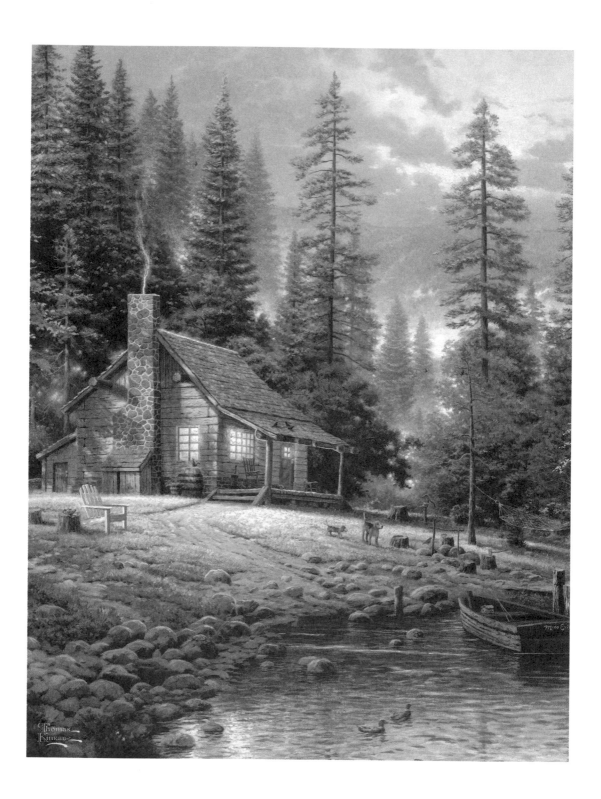

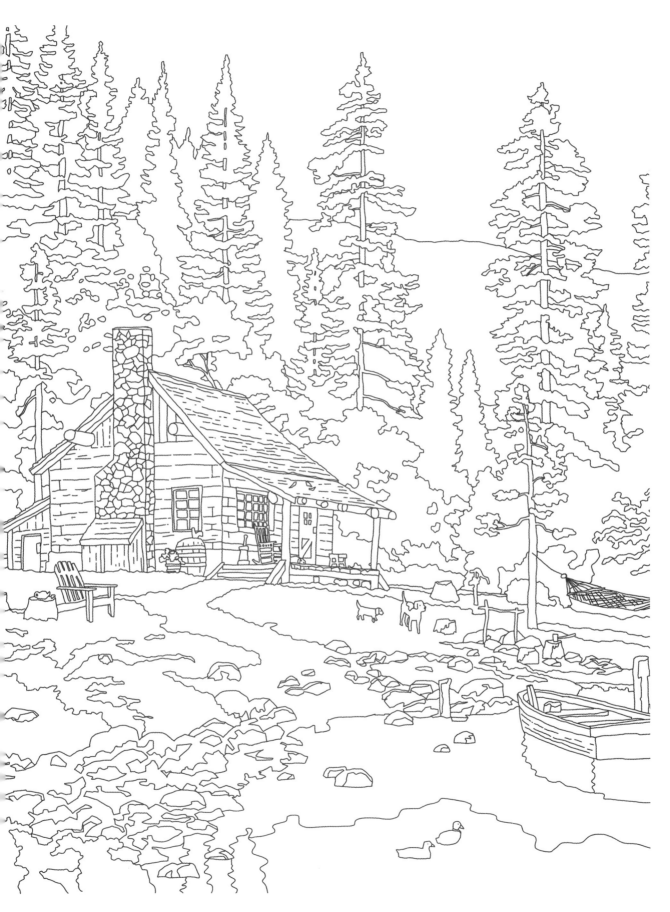

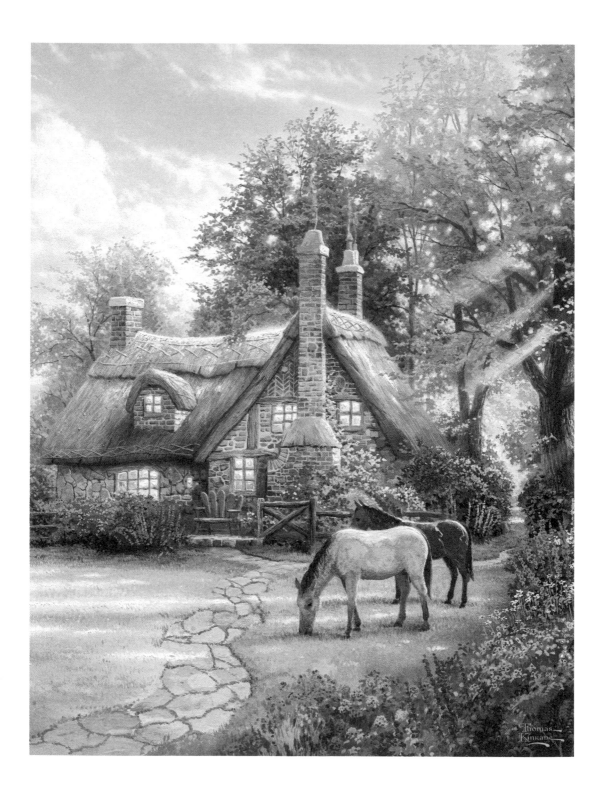

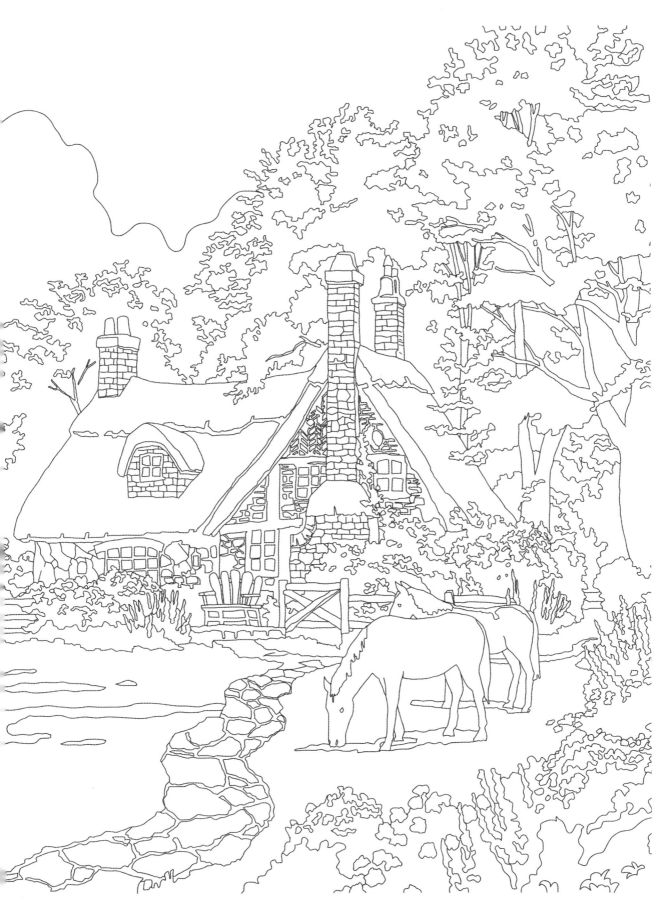

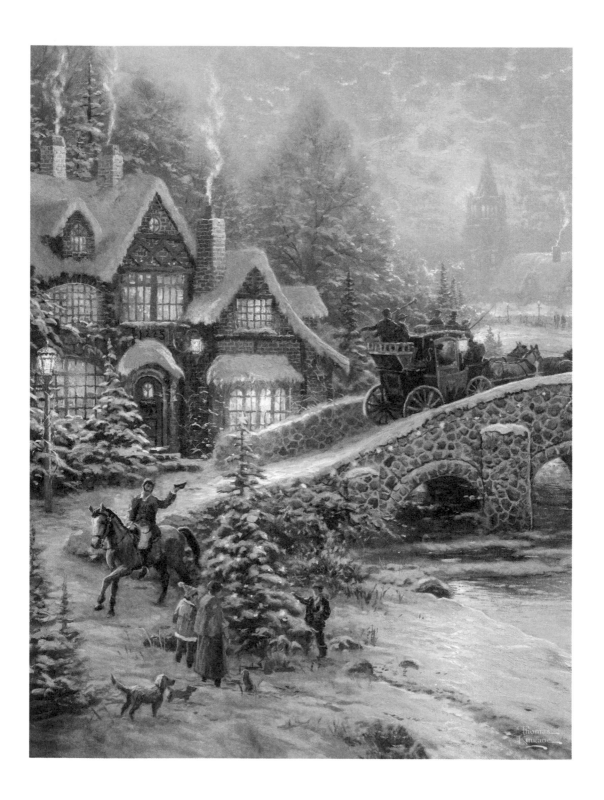

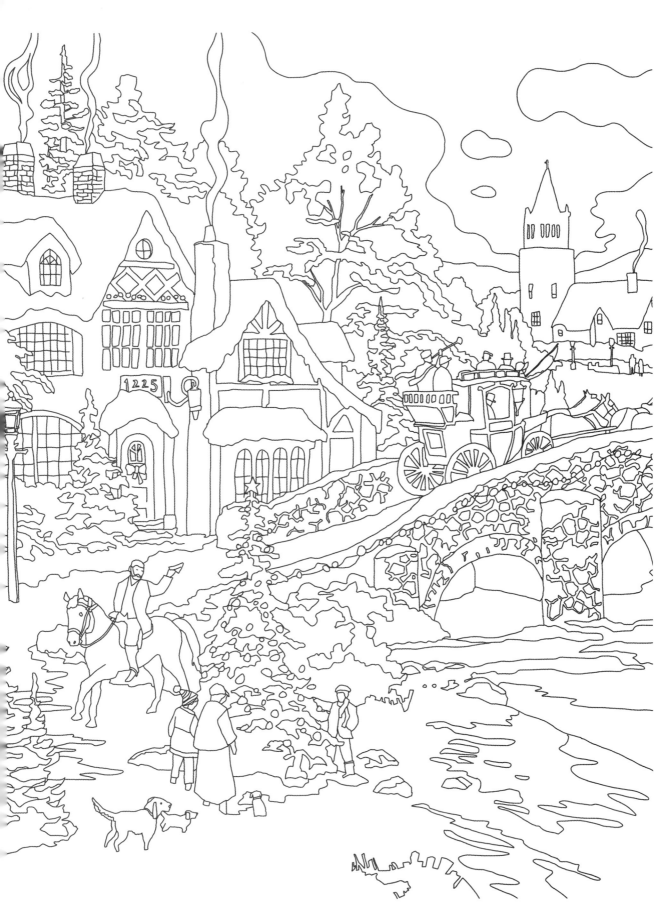

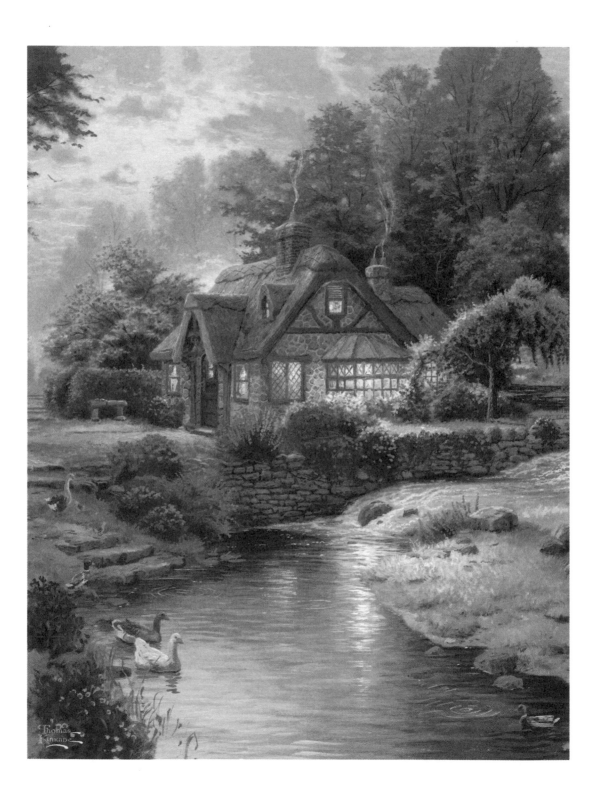

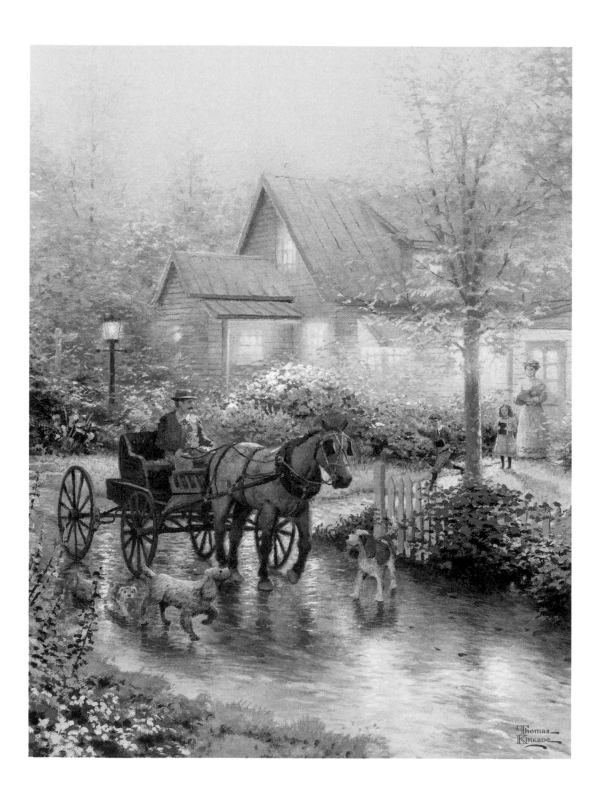

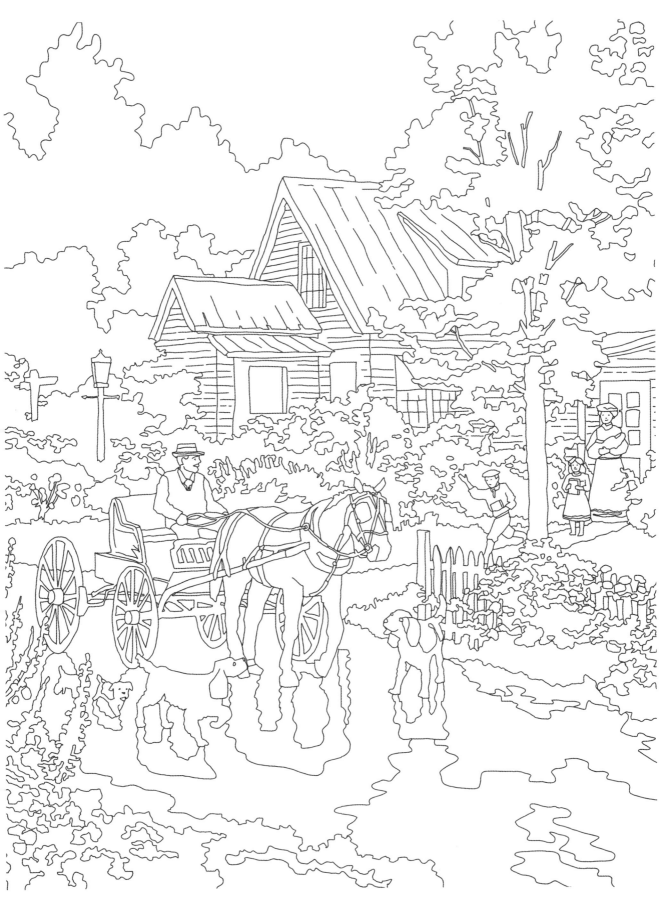

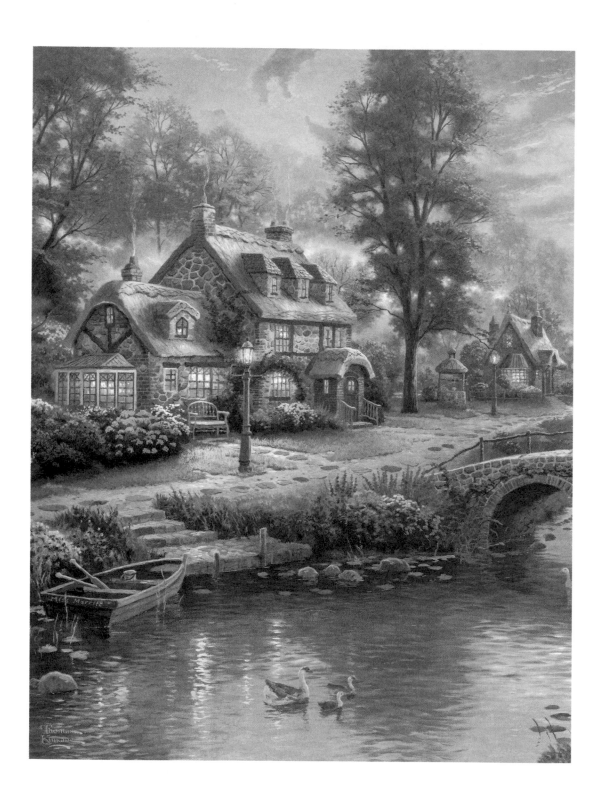

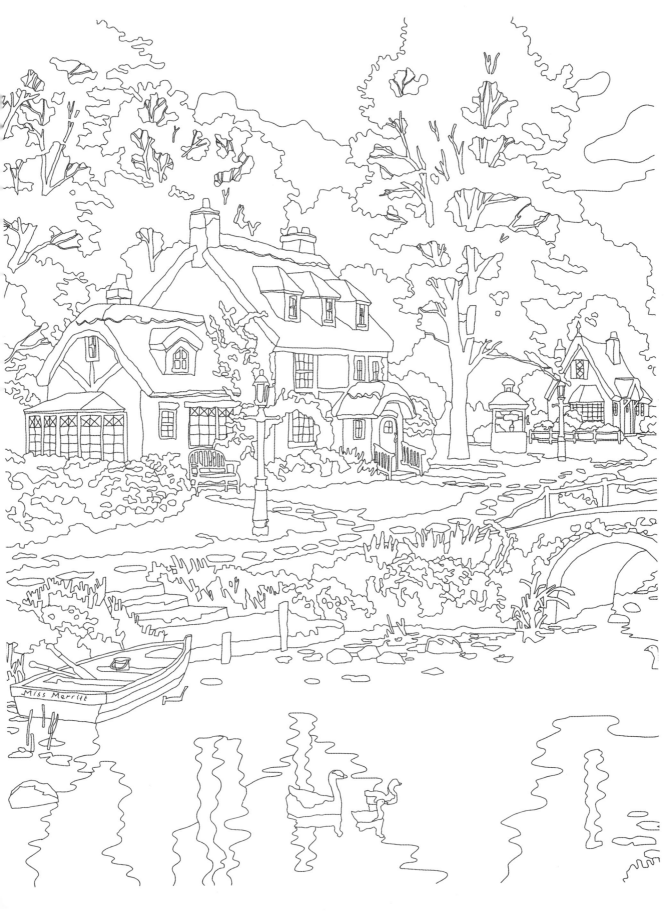

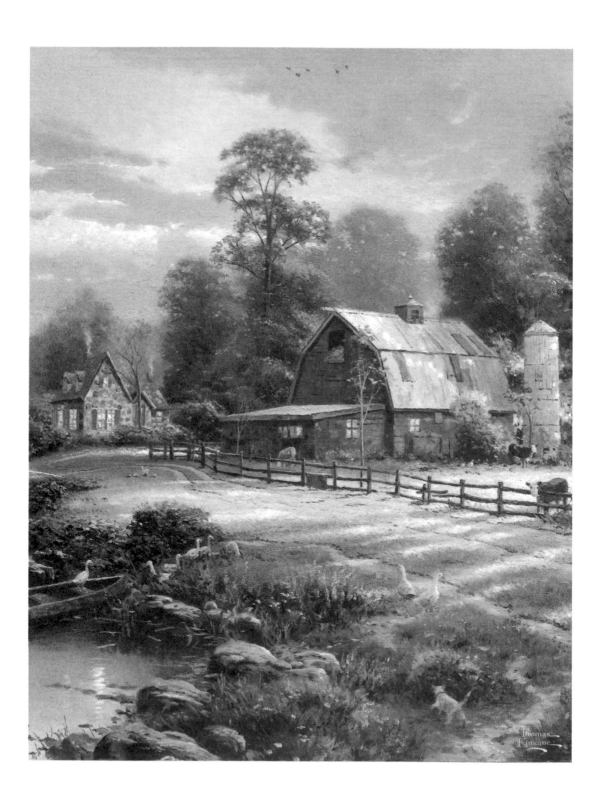

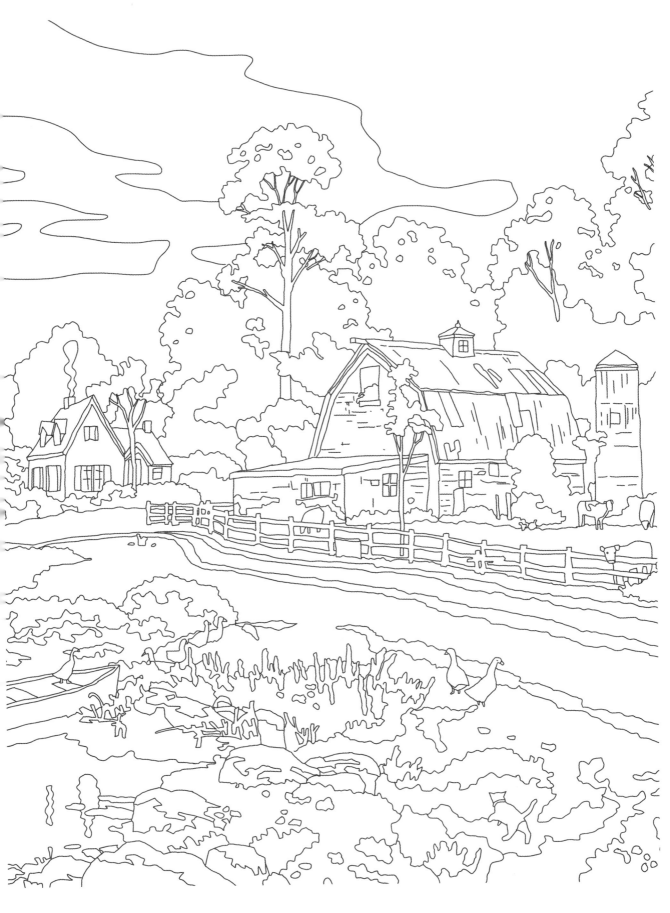

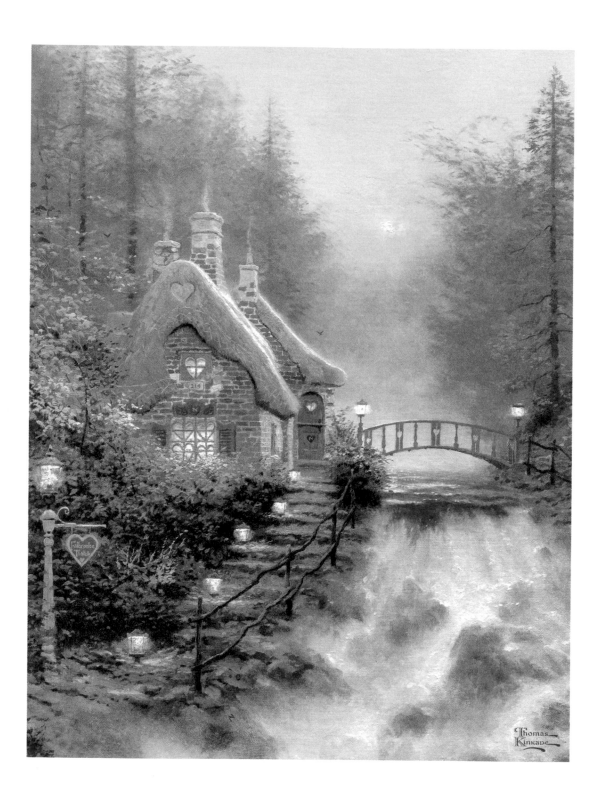

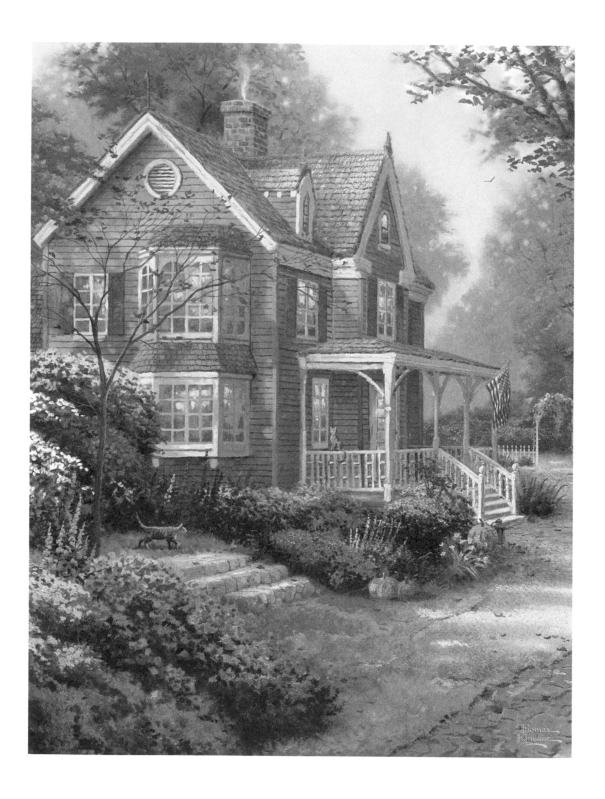

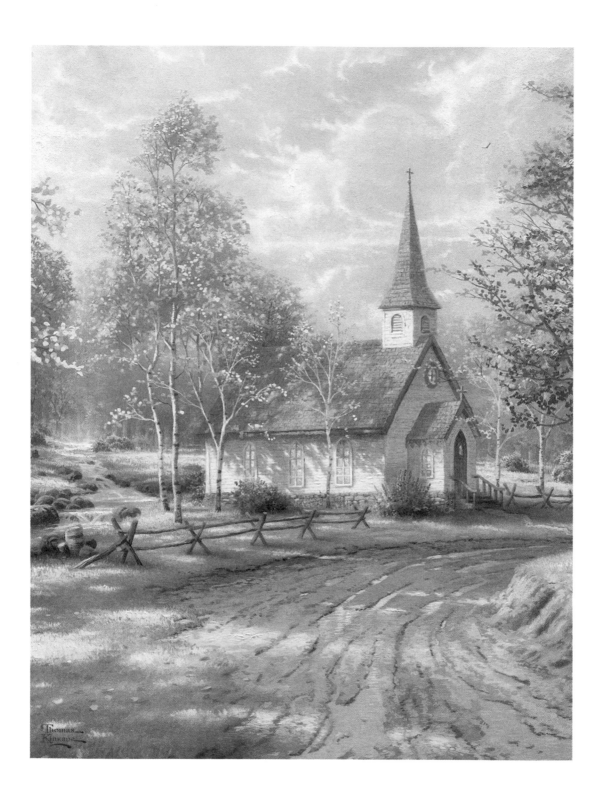

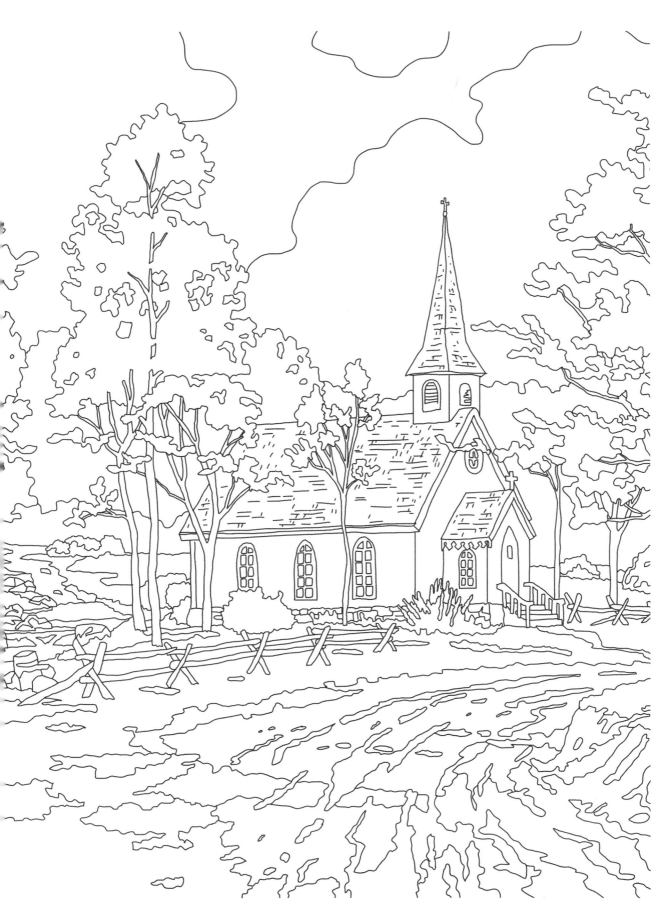

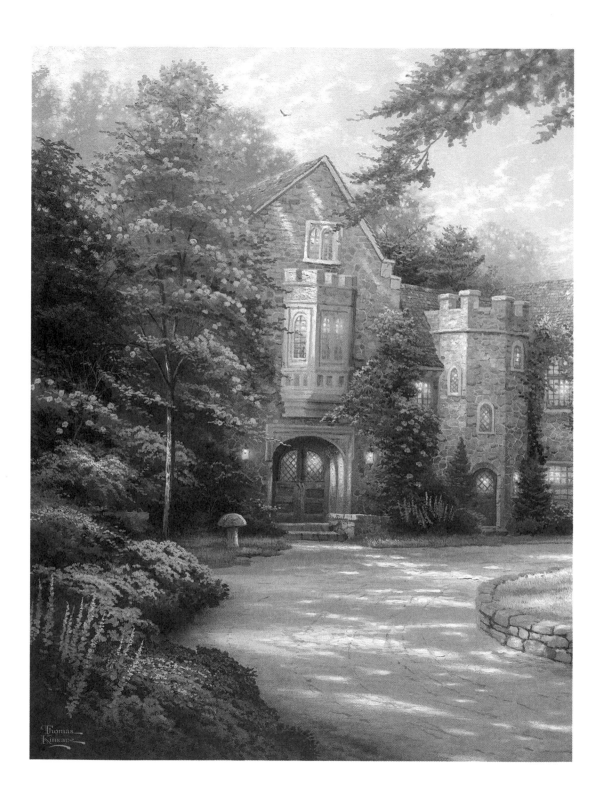

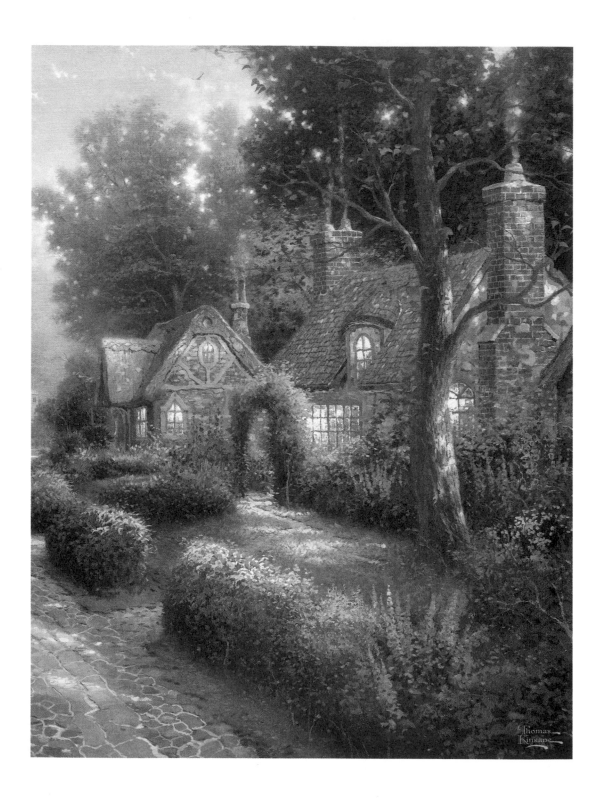

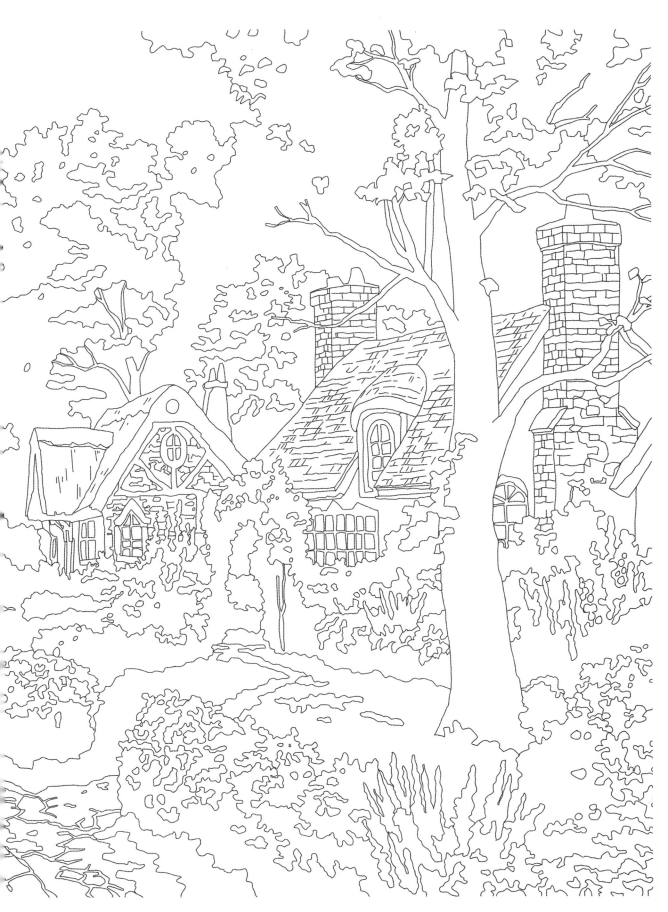

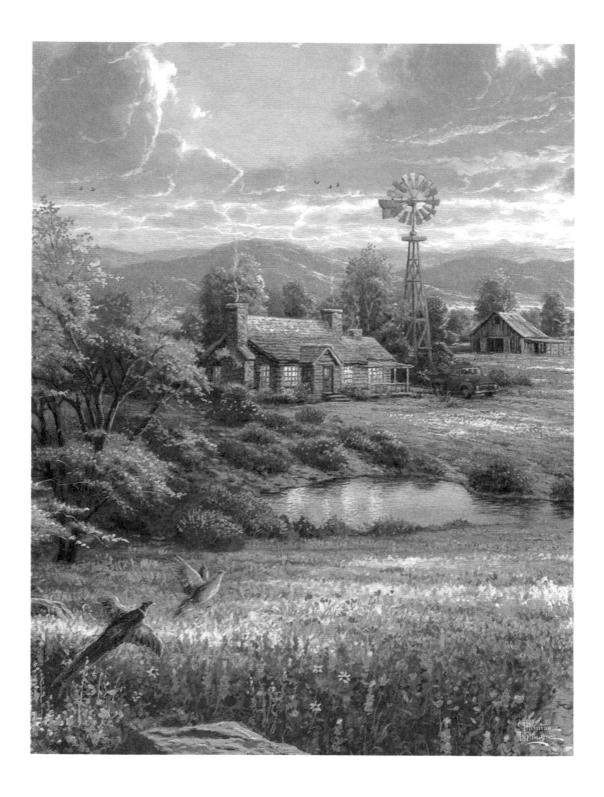

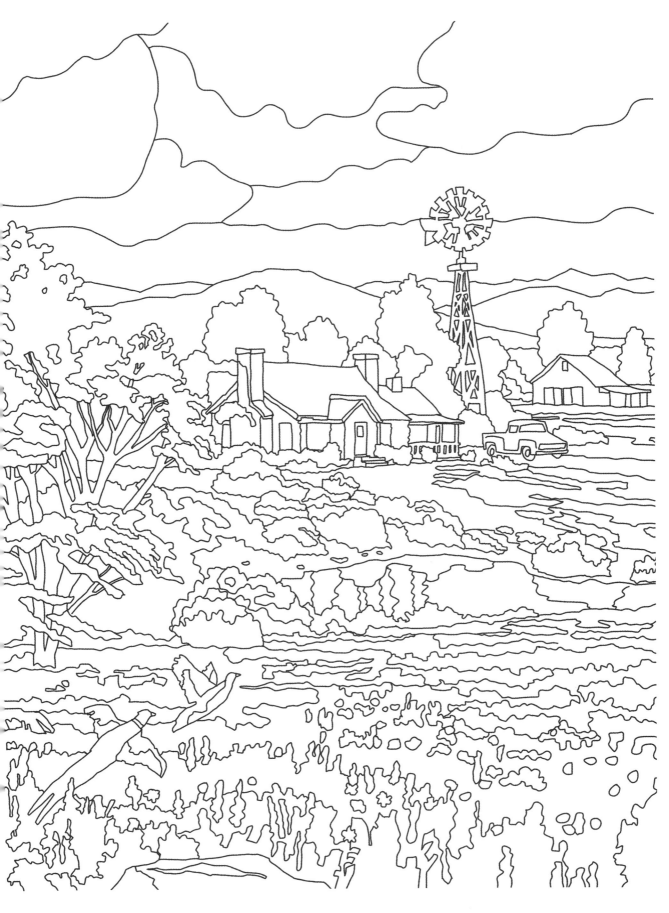

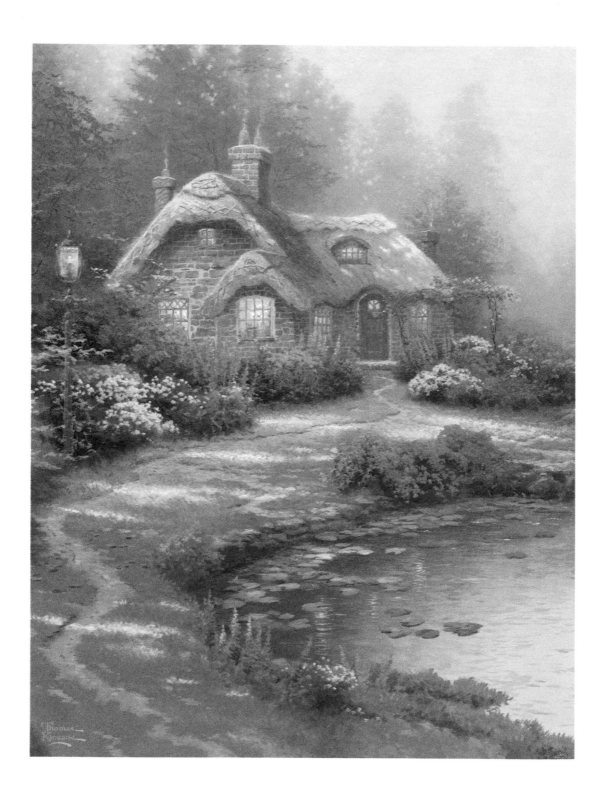

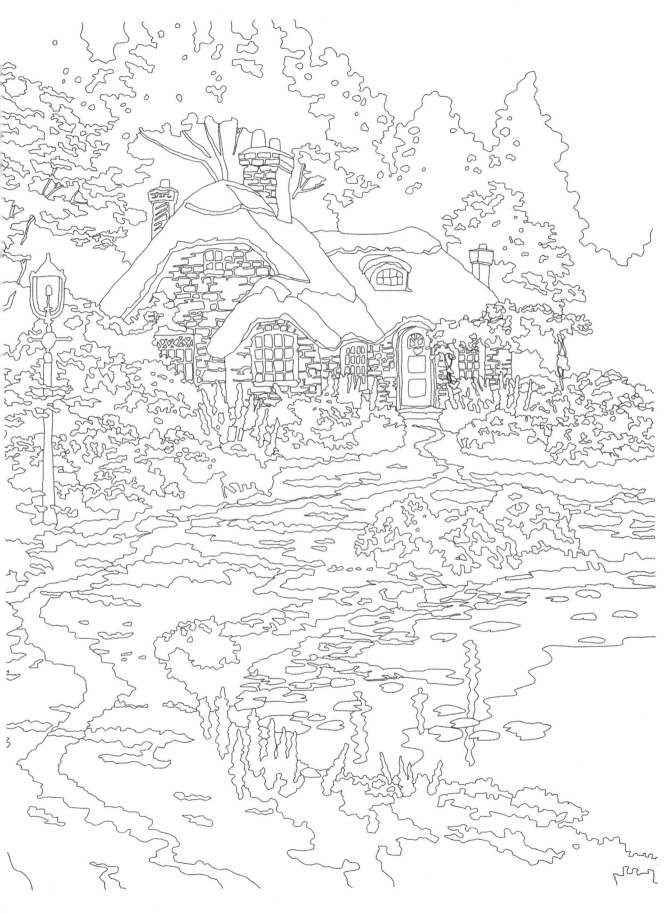

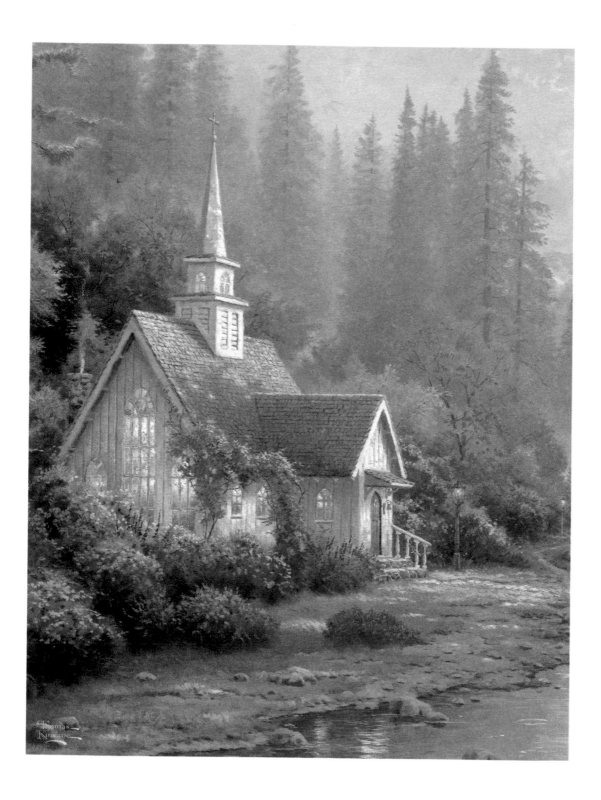

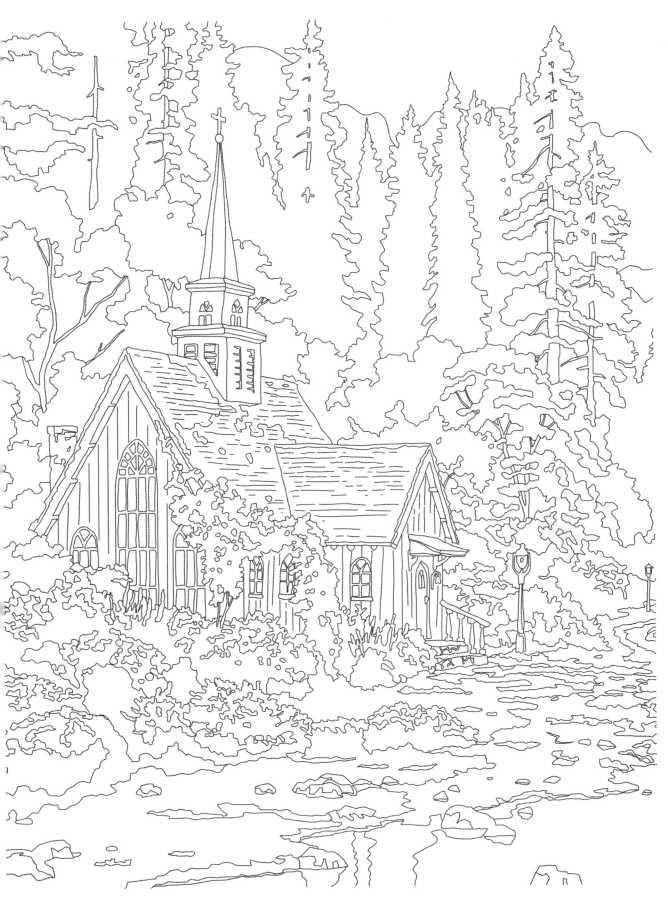

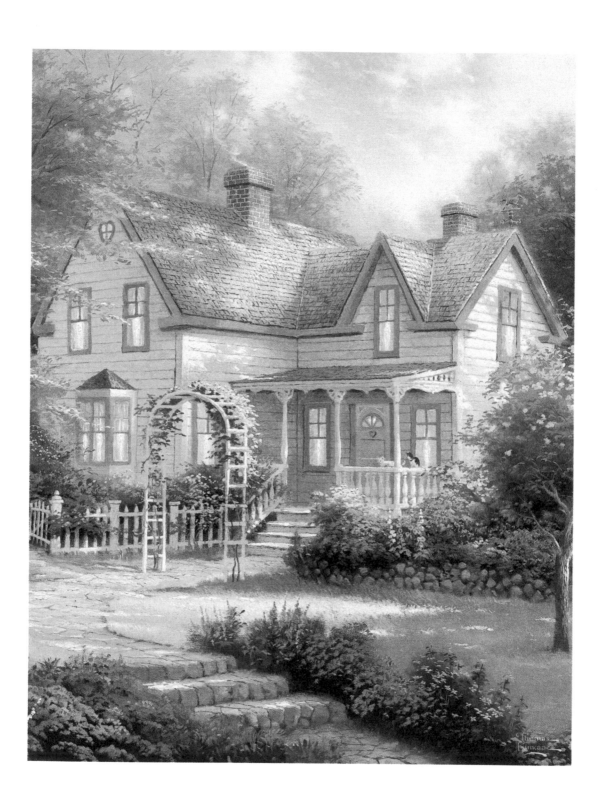

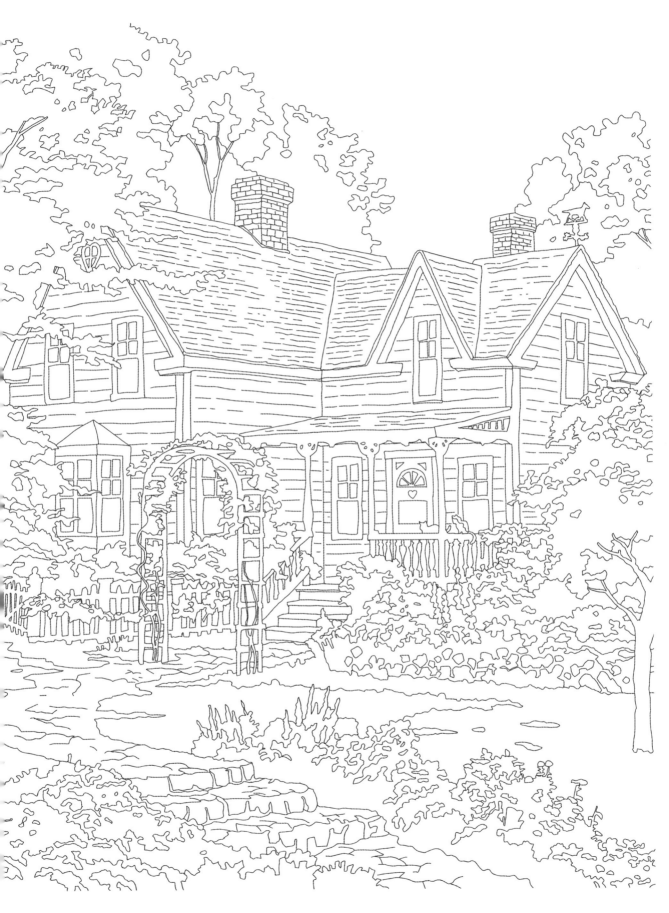

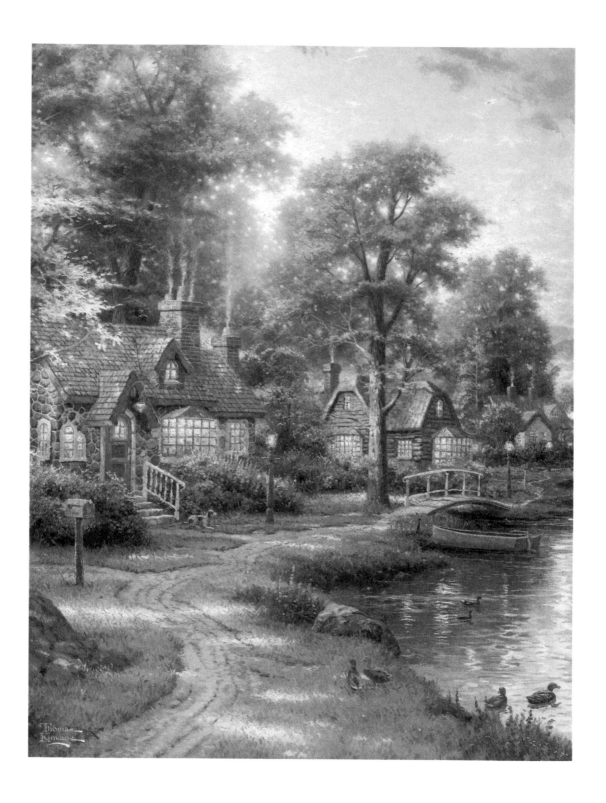

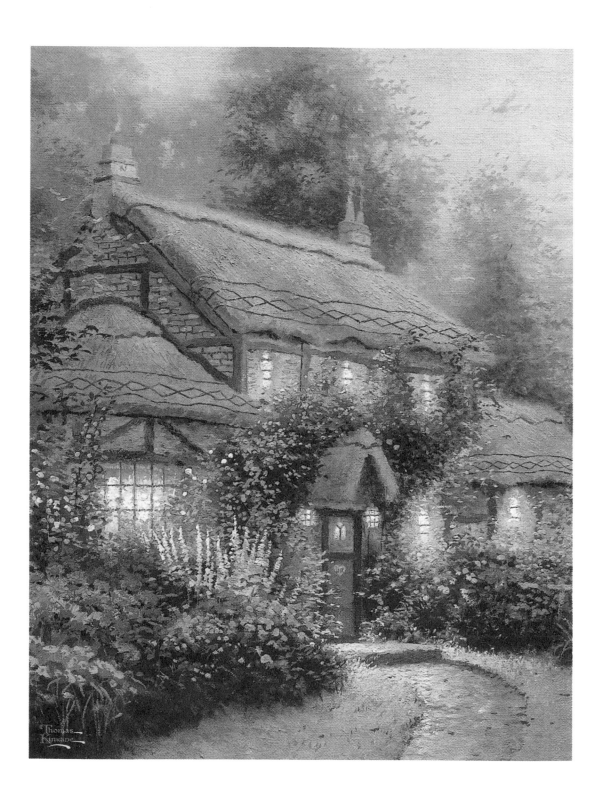

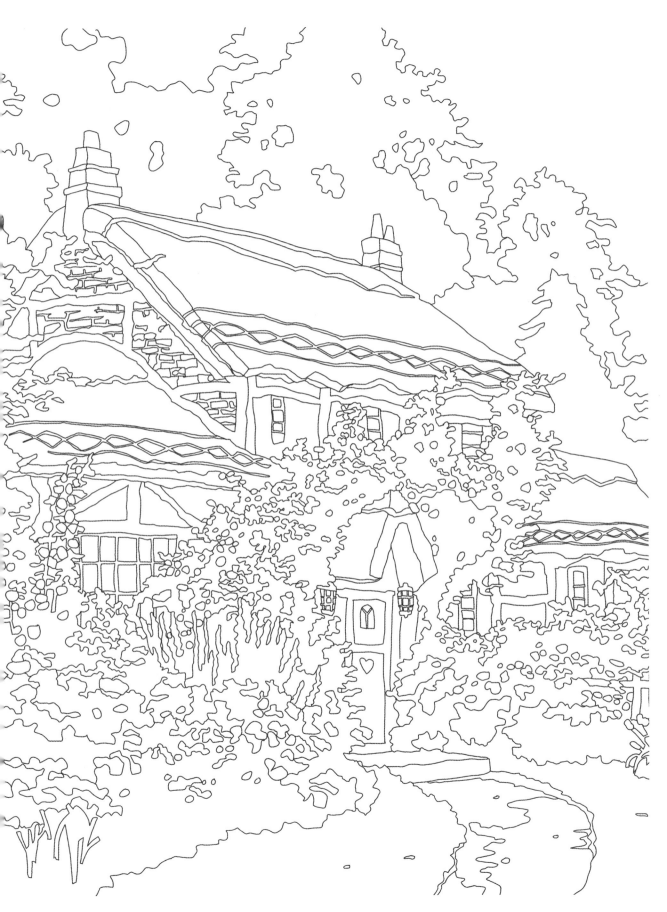

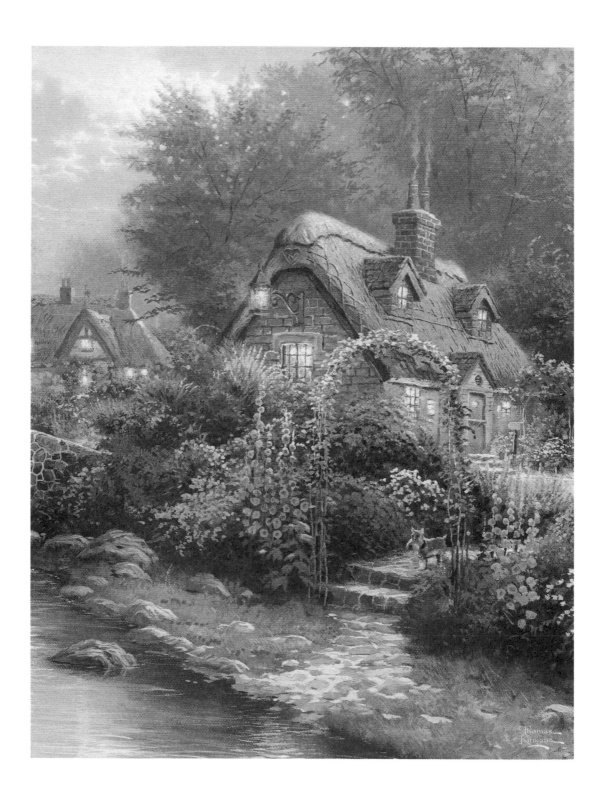

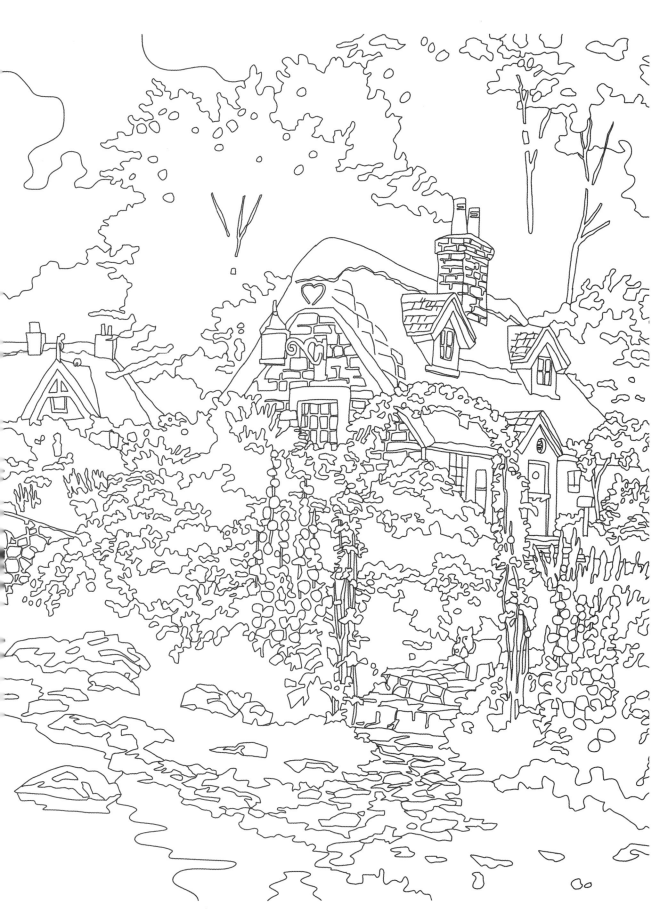

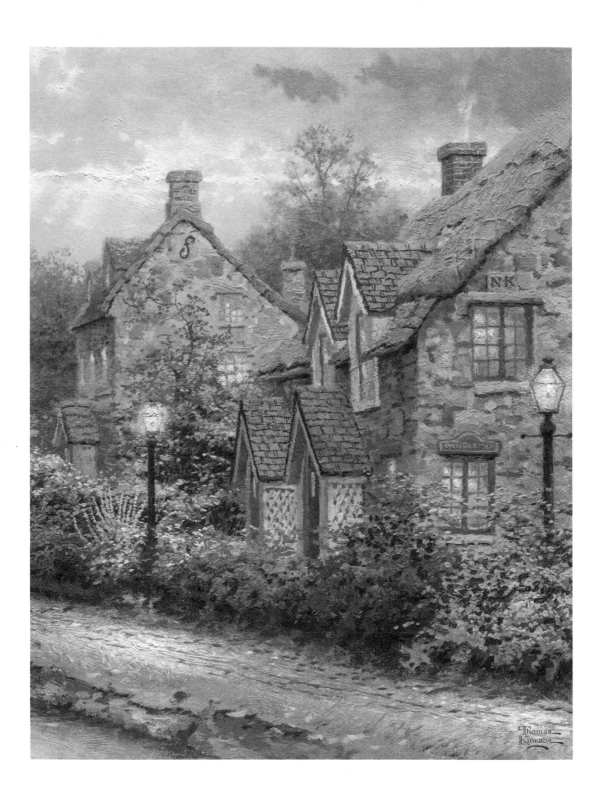

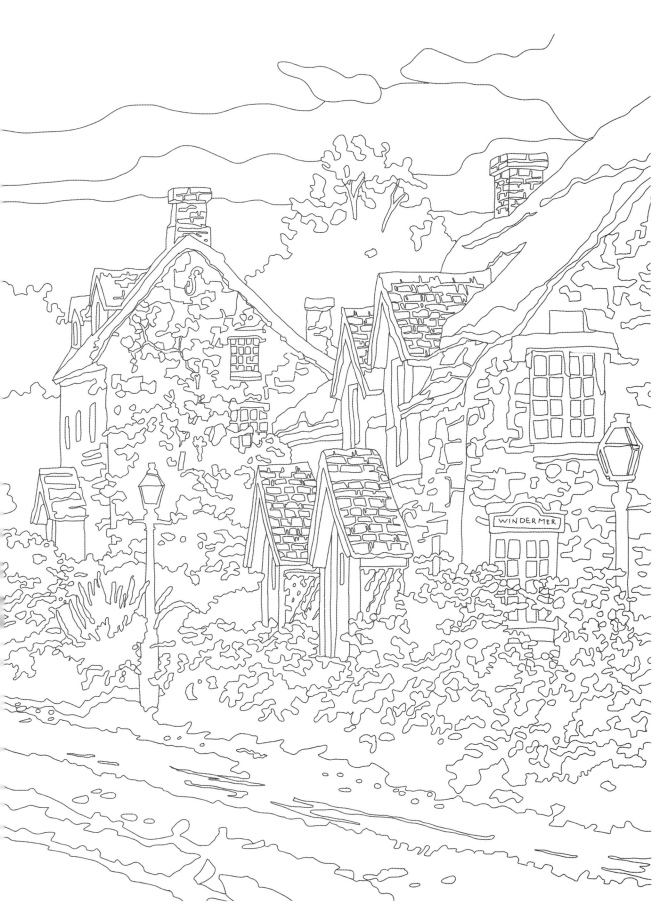

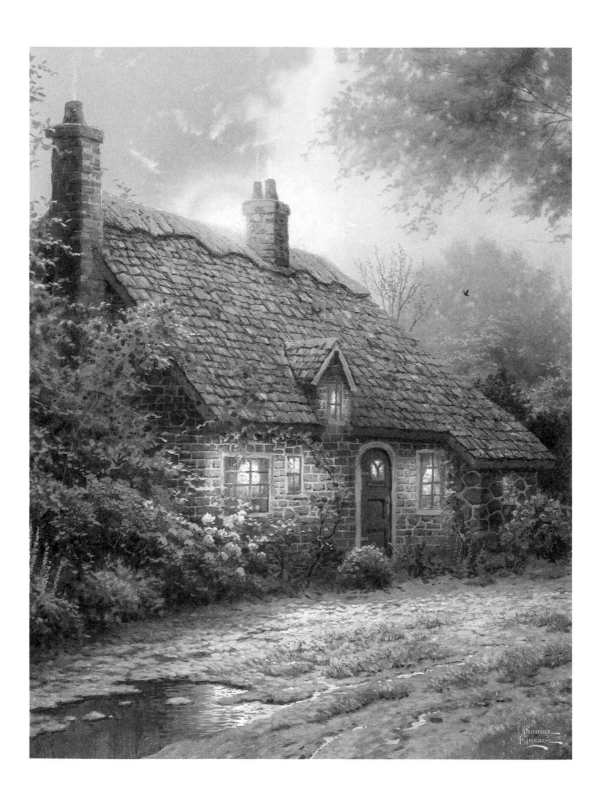

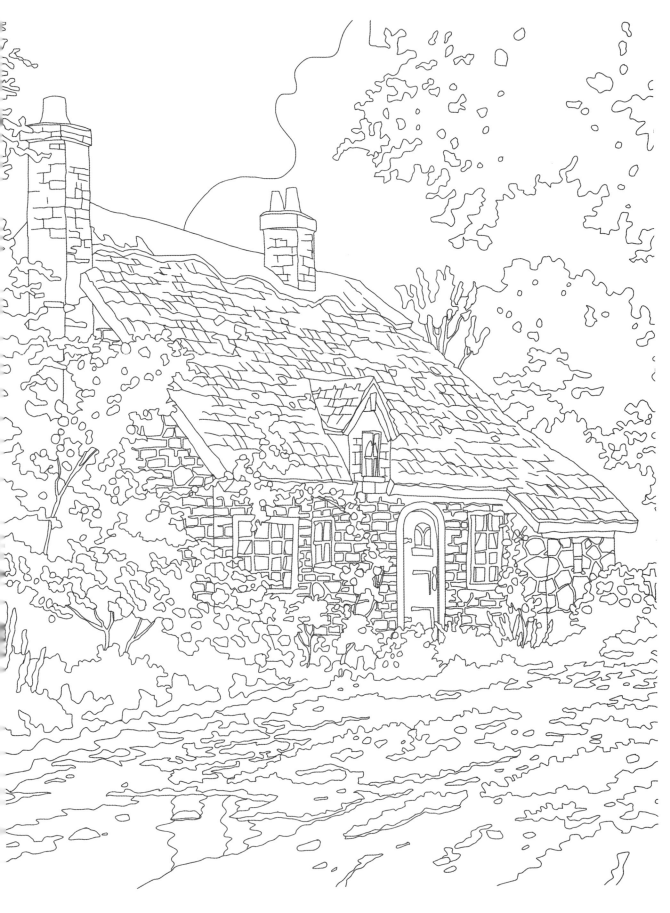

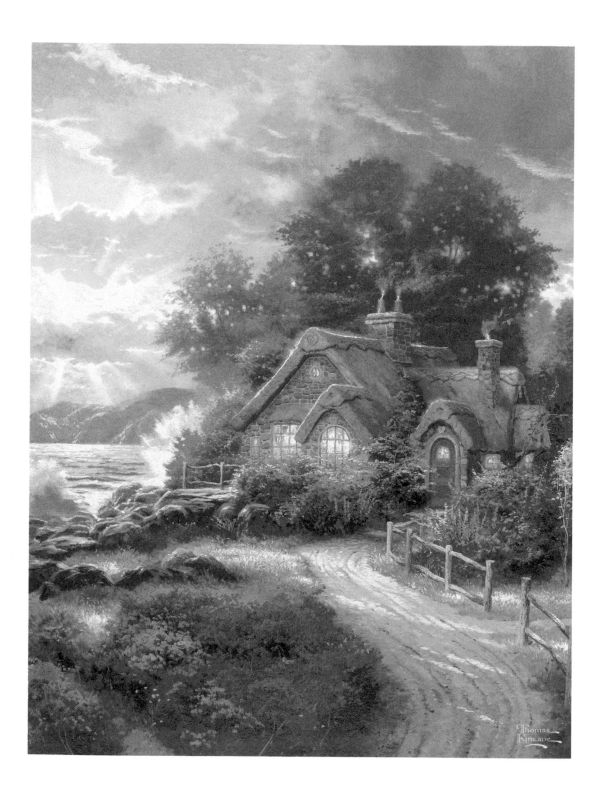

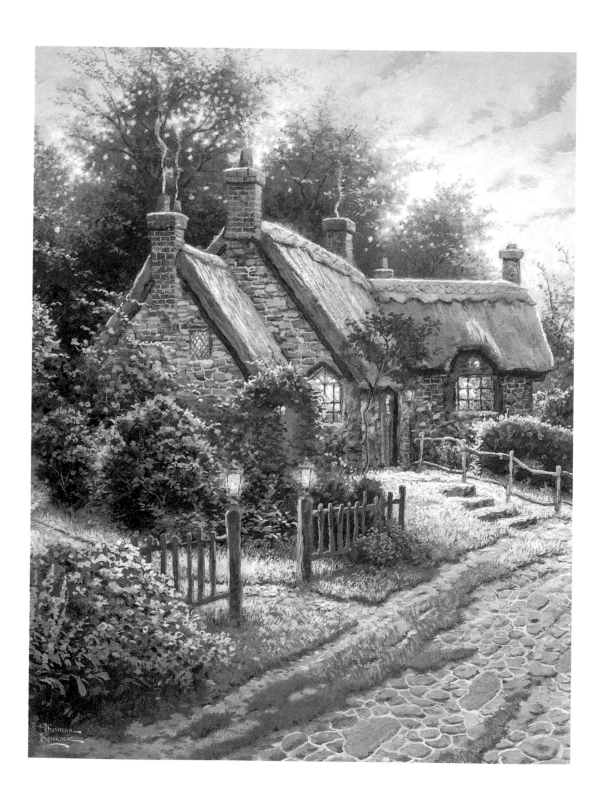

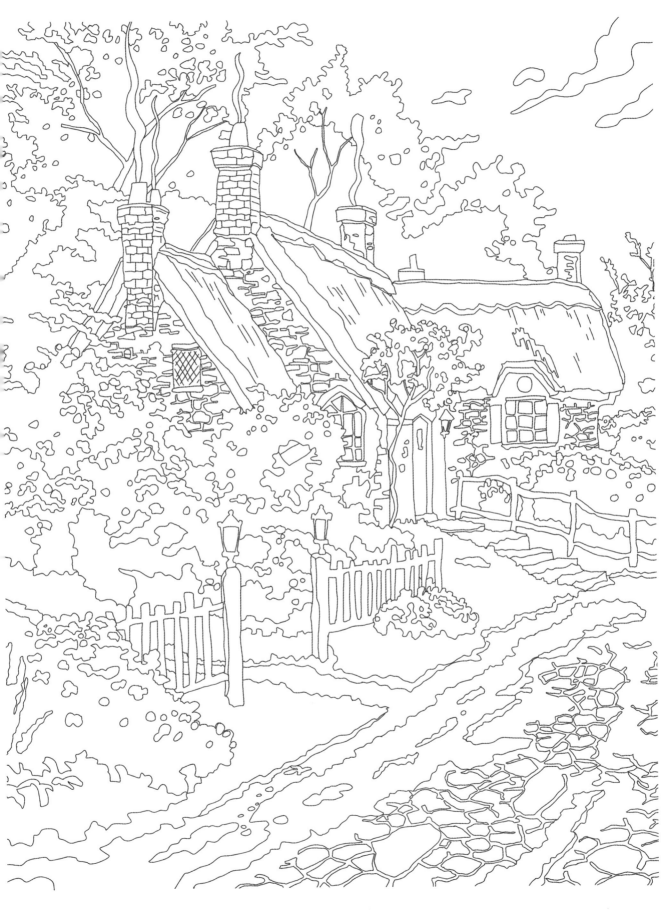

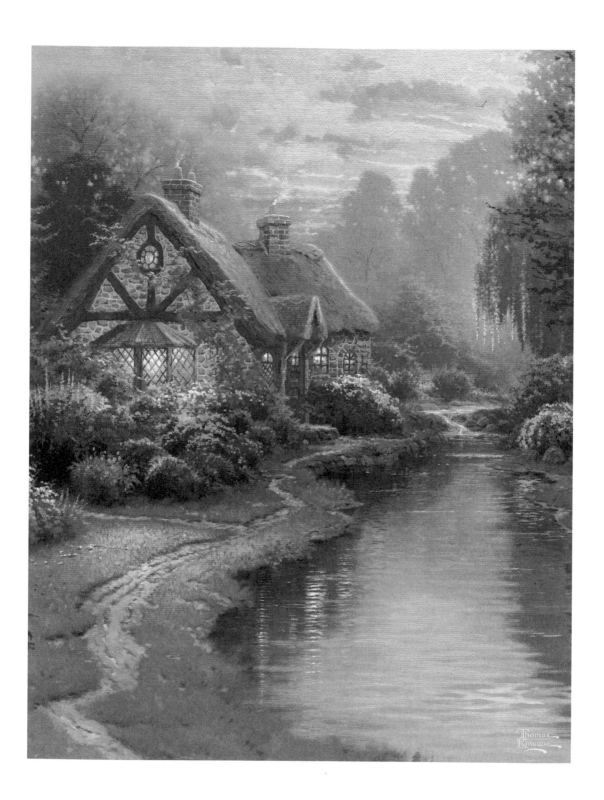

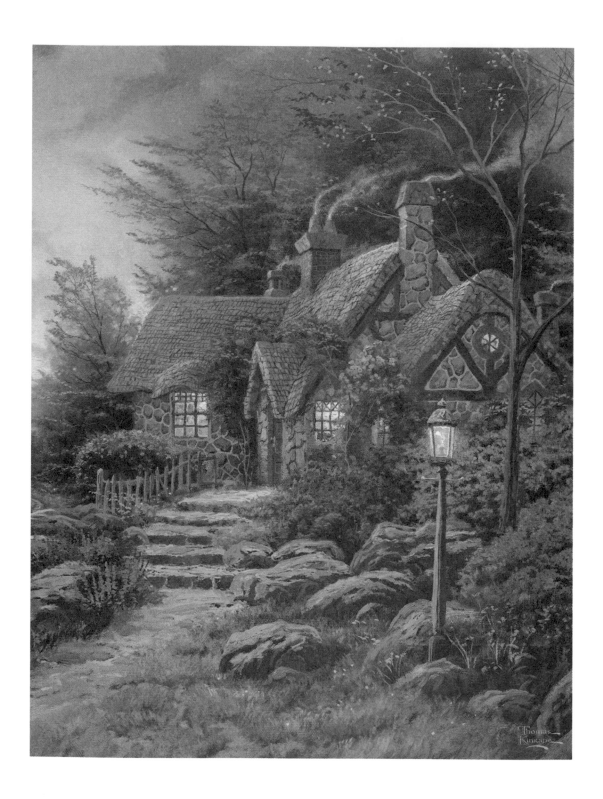

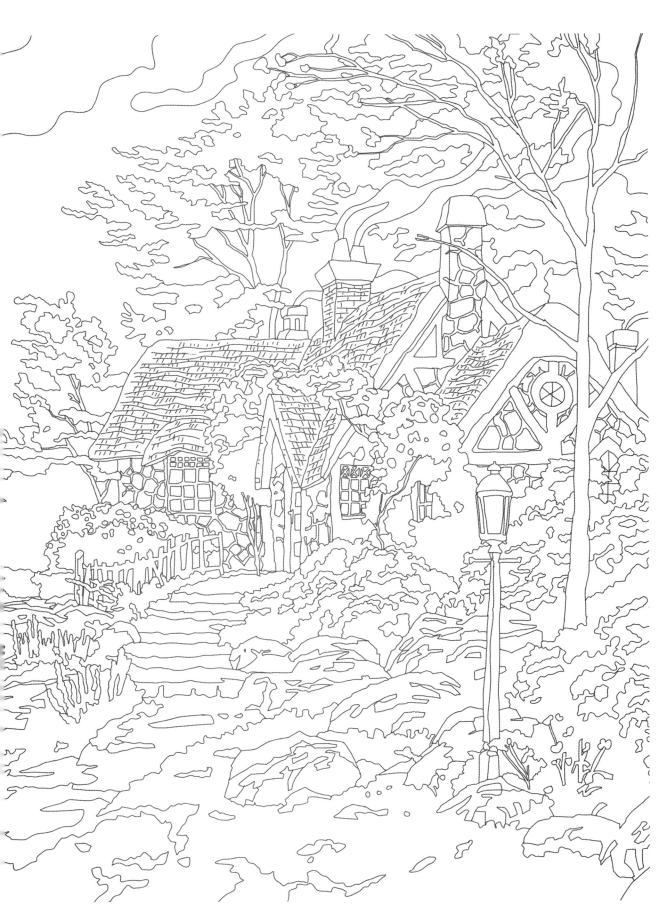

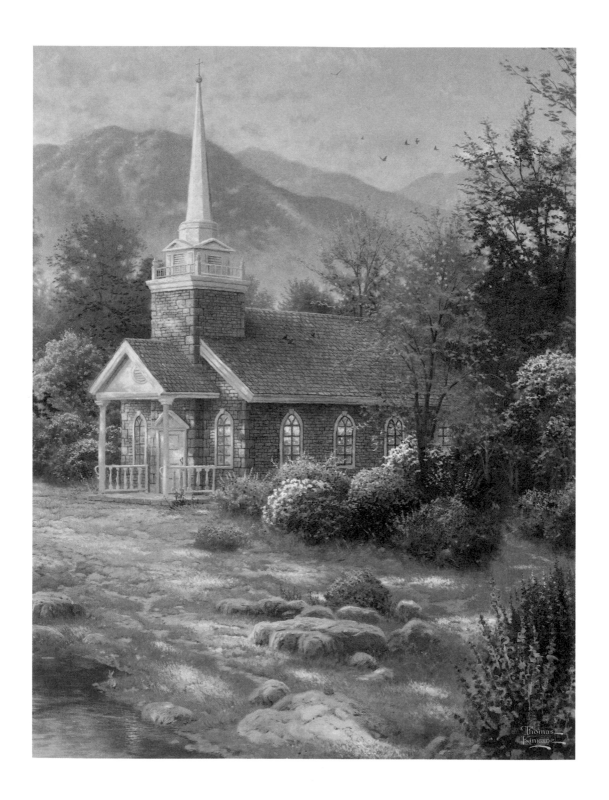

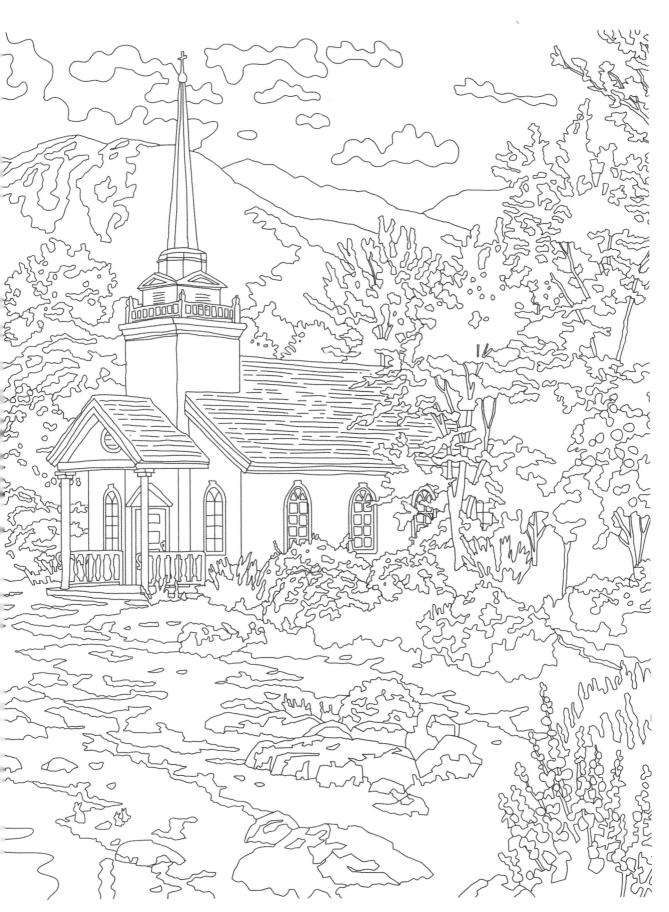

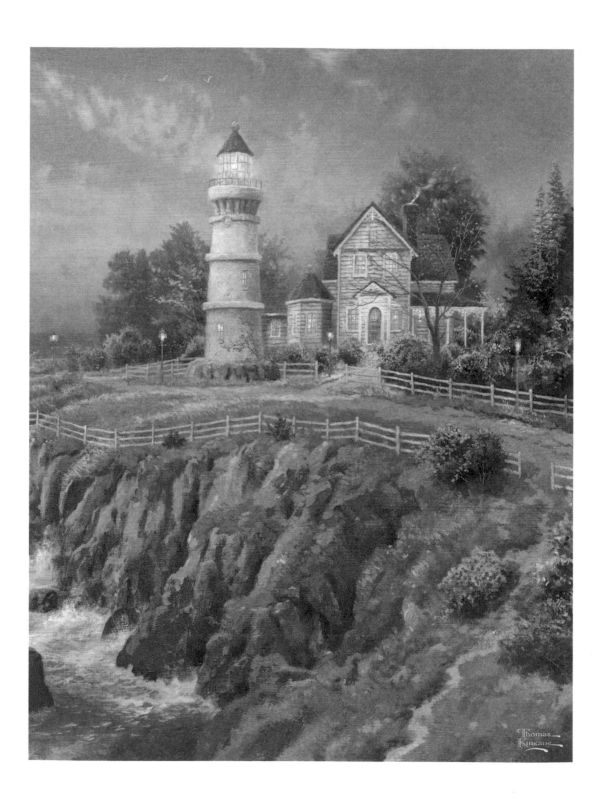

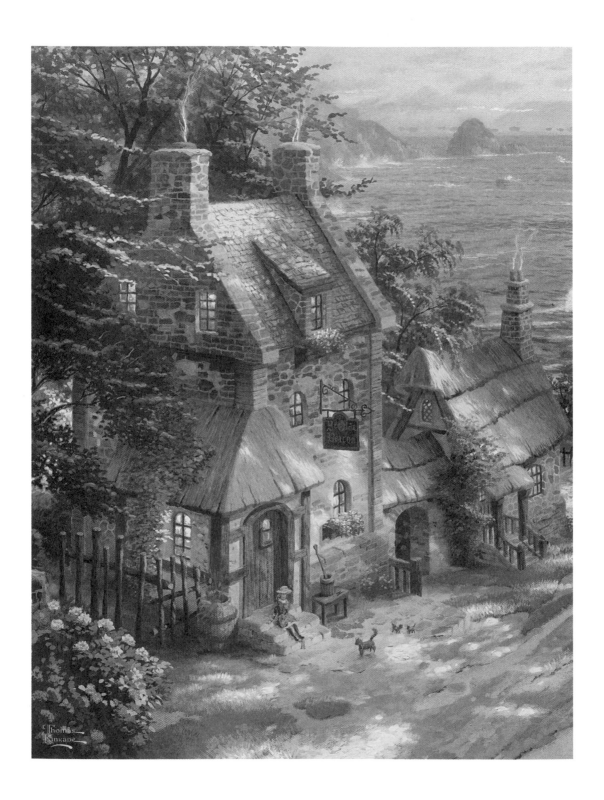

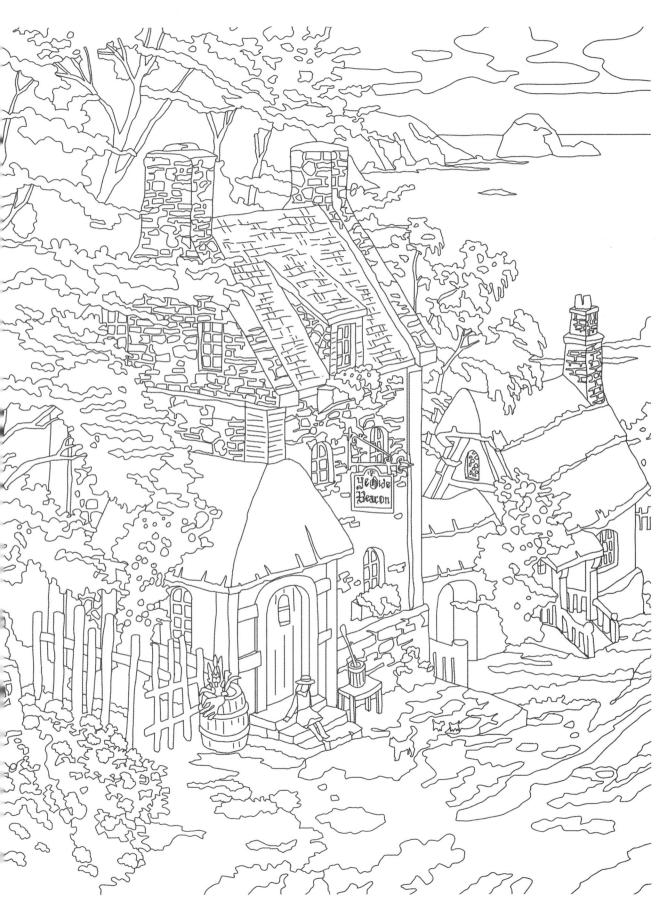

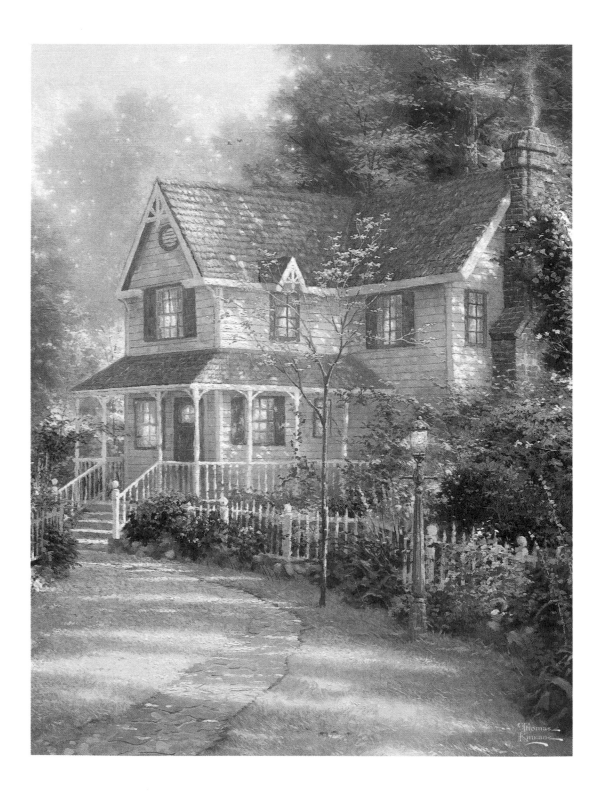

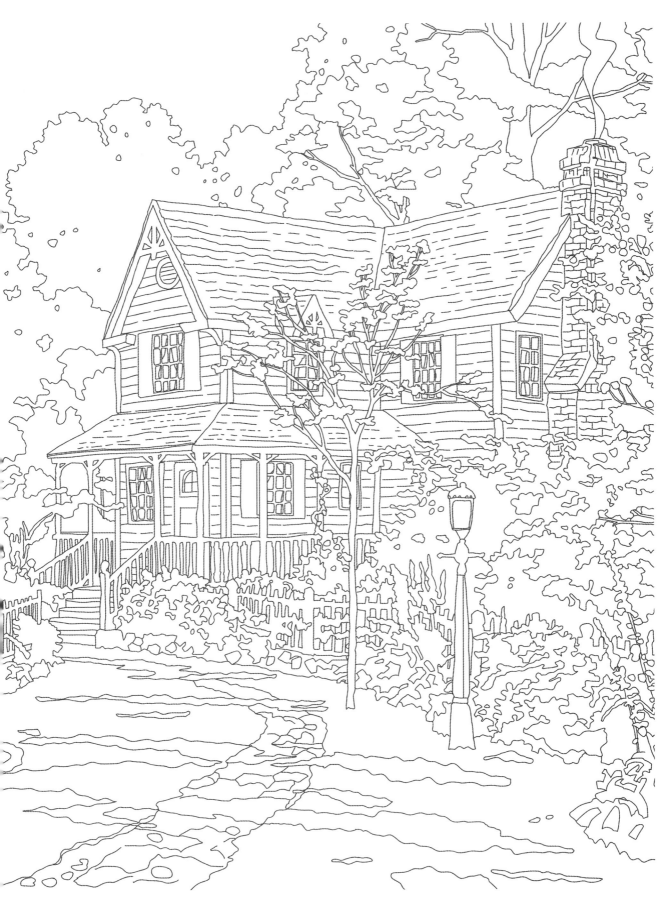

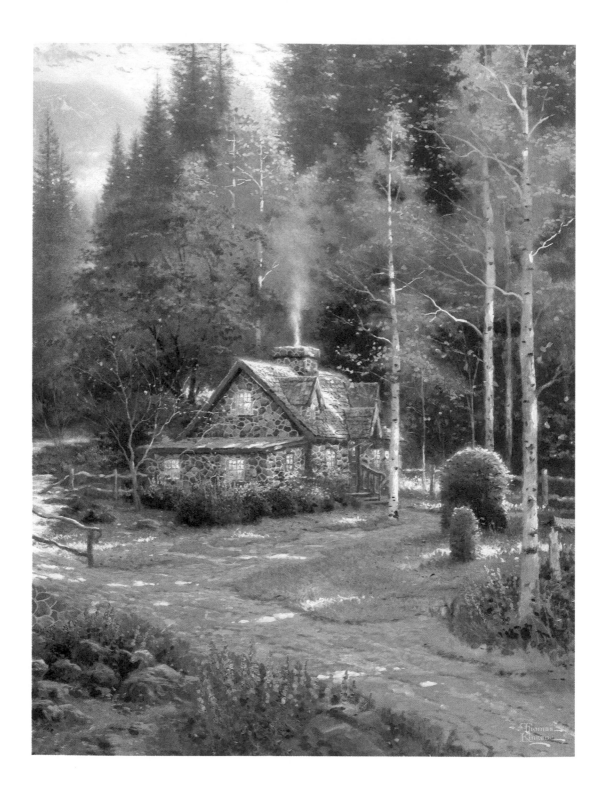

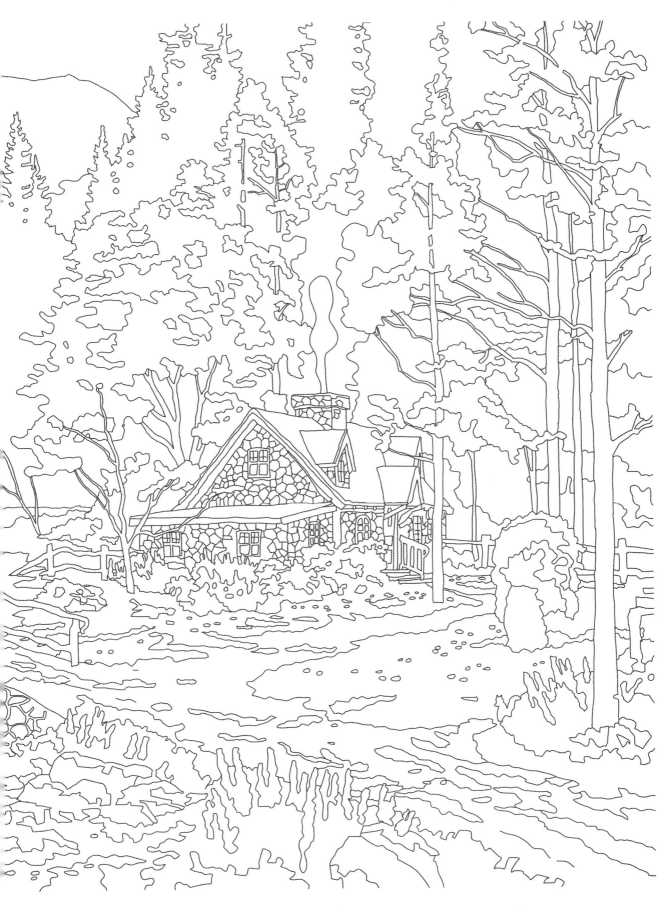

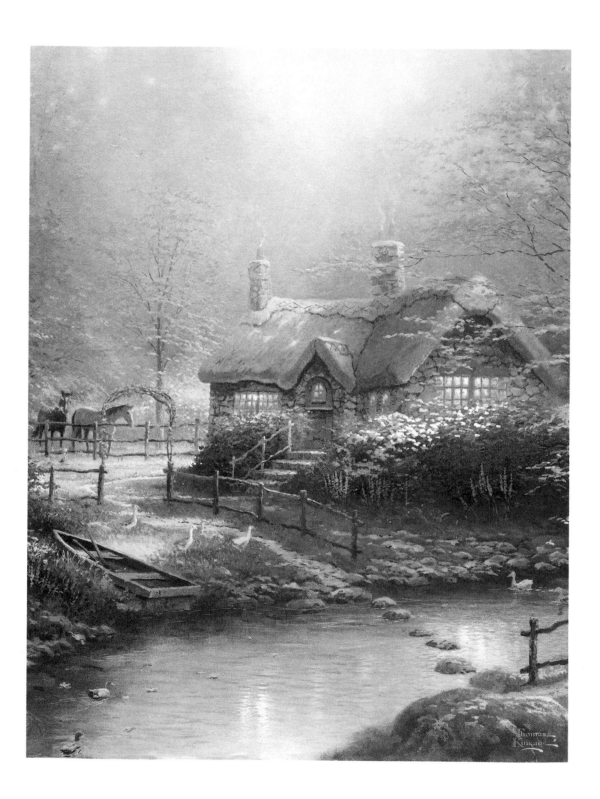

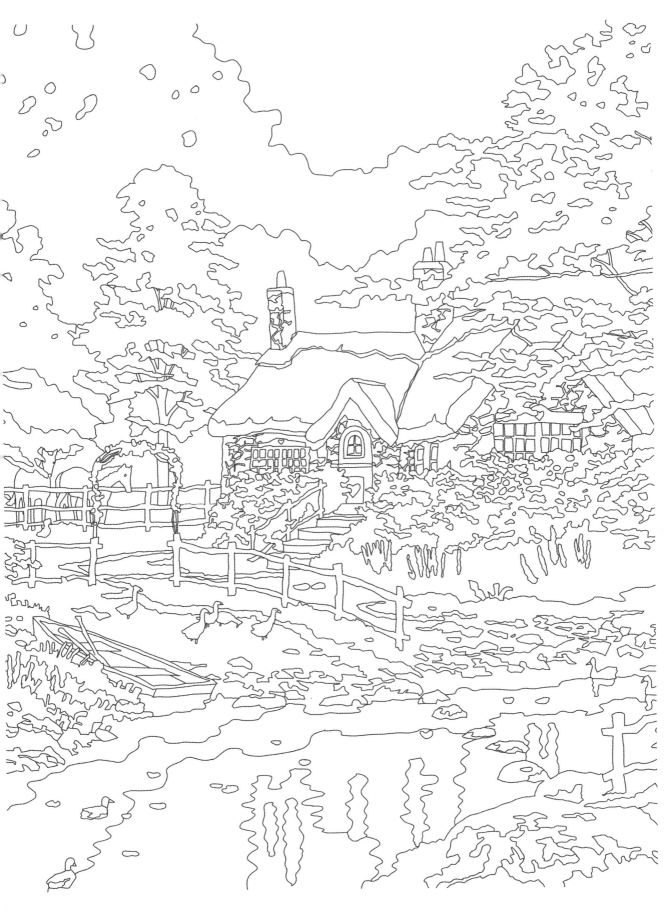

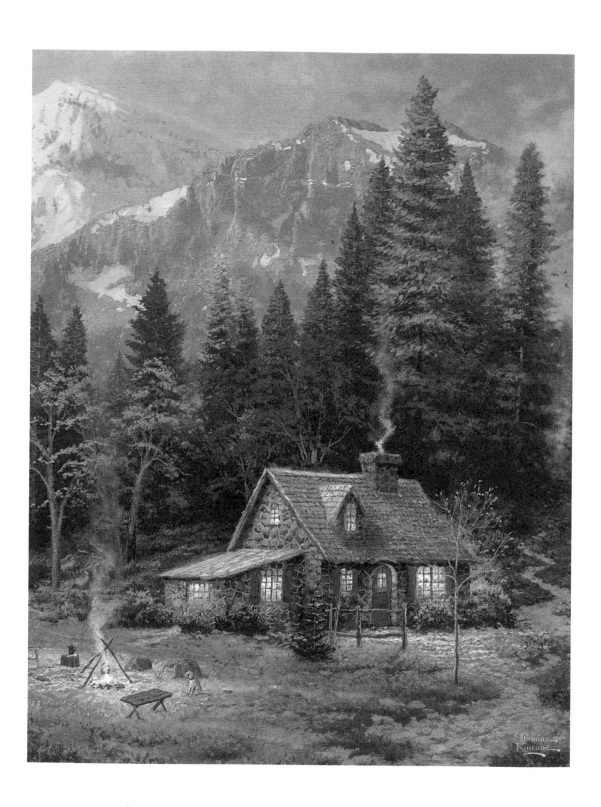

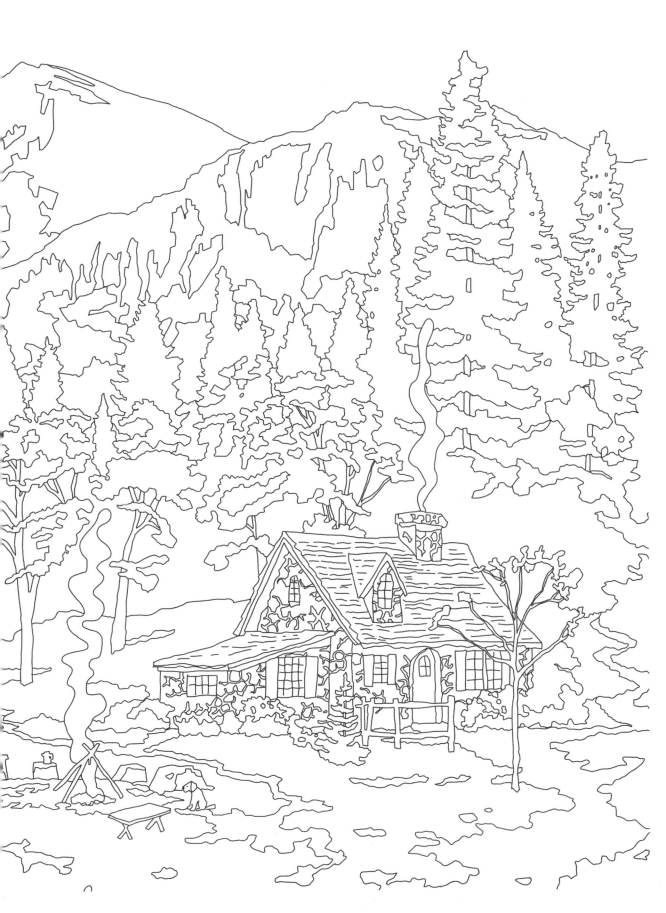

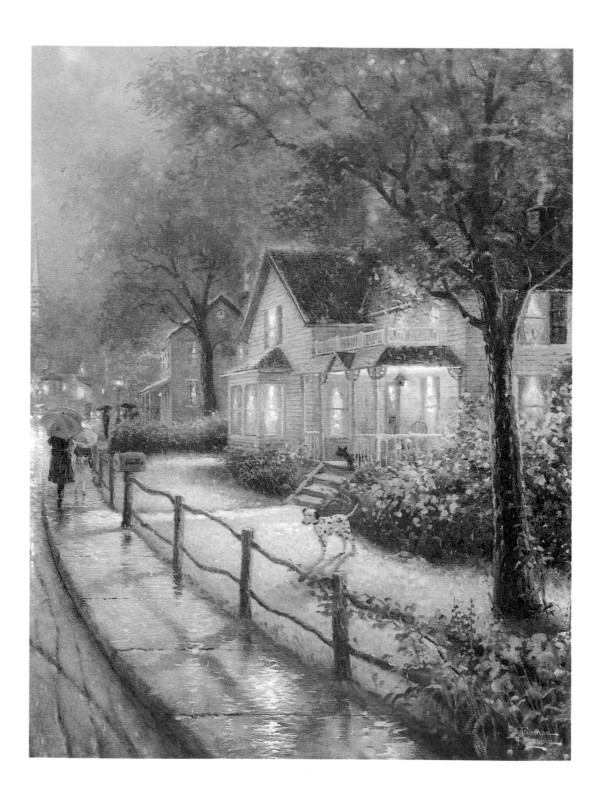

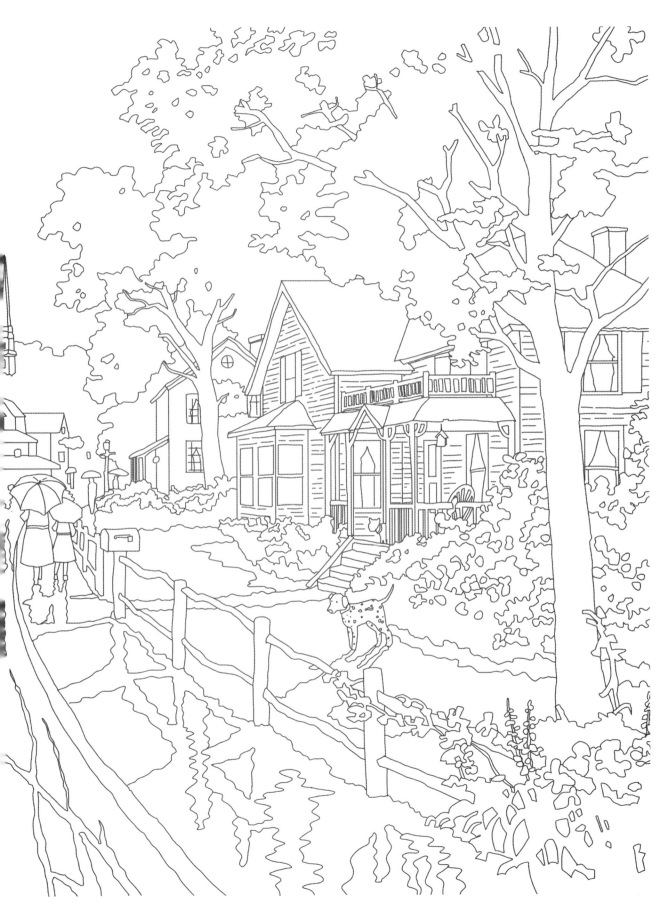

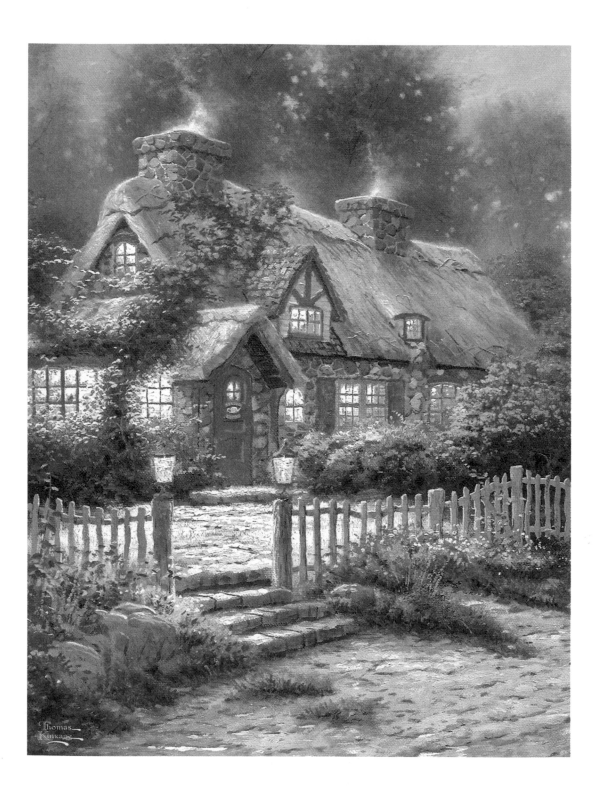

POSH® COLORING BOOK
THOMAS KINKADE DESIGNS
FOR INSPIRATION AND RELAXATION

Andrews McMeel Publishing
a division of Andrews McMeel Universal
1130 Walnut Street, Kansas City, Missouri 64106

www.andrewsmcmeel.com

16 17 18 19 20 QGR 10 9 8 7 6 5 4

ISBN: 978-1-4494-7887-2

ATTENTION: SCHOOLS AND BUSINESSES
Andrews McMeel books are available at quantity discounts
with bulk purchase for educational, business, or sales
promotional use. For information, please e-mail the Andrews
McMeel Publishing Special Sales Department:
specialsales@amuniversal.com.